CONTENTS

DIRECTOR GENERAL'S STATEMENT

1994 was a milestone in the regulation of the water industry. During the year we undertook the first major review of price limits. Companies are focusing on cutting costs and improving efficiency. Customers are now seeing a slowing down in the rate at which their bills are increasing and for some their water bills are falling in real terms. Large investment programmes, particularly for the treatment of sewage, are bringing environmental benefits. Without these environmental programmes bills would be falling in relation to prices generally.

The Periodic Review

On 28 July 1994 I announced the outcome of the first Periodic Review. Price limits for the 31 companies in England and Wales were reset simultaneously to a published timetable.

Ian Byatt, Director General

Parliament required me to ensure that companies have a sound financial basis for carrying out their obligations. Subject to that, I must protect customers and promote economy and efficiency. I have to balance different duties and satisfy various interests.

I emphasised the need to develop processes which were fair and open to all concerned. I consulted widely on the approach. Companies were given opportunities to set out their position. The Government and the quality regulators were invited to set out the quality dimension. My decisions and the reasoning behind them were published in *Future Charges for Water and Sewerage Services.*

The new price limits represented the culmination of three years' hard work by the companies, the quality regulators and Ofwat. The Review was carried out effectively at much lower cost than was incurred in setting the original price limits in 1989.

We delivered results which were acceptable to customers and manageable by companies.

Acceptable to customers

The new price limits fell within the range which I had felt customers could accept as reasonable, taking into account the scale of environmental obligations faced by the companies - particularly those arising from the EC Urban Waste Water Treatment Directive adopted by the UK in 1991.

1994 REPORT *of the* DIRECTOR GENERAL *of* WATER SERVICES

FOR THE PERIOD 1 APRIL 1994 TO 31 MARCH 1995

To

RT. HON JOHN SELWYN GUMMER, MP

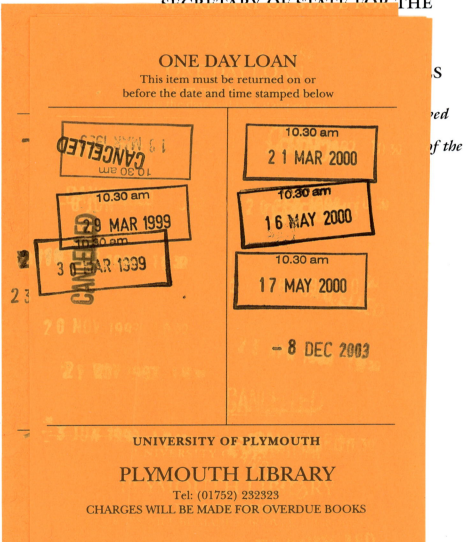

Section 193 of the Water Industry Act 1991

Ordered by the House of Commons to be printed
21 June 1995

LONDON: HMSO

£11.75 net

It is a mistake to think that profit, in the sense of a surplus over cost, has any special or unique connection with capitalism. On the contrary, it must be the rationale of business activity in any society, whether capitalist or socialist, which is growing and dynamic.

C A R Crosland
The Future of Socialism 1956

Customers of most of the water only companies will see their water bills fall in real terms over the next ten years. If it were not for the scale of environmental obligations facing the water and sewerage companies, their customers would also see bills falling.

I involved customer representatives closely in setting prices. The chairmen of the ten Customer Service Committees advised me on customers' views and concerns from a position of knowledge. I intend to build on this valuable innovation in regulation.

After the Review I asked all the companies to publish documents to tell their customers exactly what service improvements they could expect to see over the coming years. These public documents followed the Market Plans (published by the companies in the Spring of 1994) in involving and explaining to customers what they pay for.

Manageable by companies

Only two companies asked me to refer them to the Monopolies and Mergers Commission (MMC) because they thought the price limits were too low - South West Water Services Ltd and Portsmouth Water plc. The MMC have until 28 June to redetermine these price limits.

The new price limits allow the companies to maintain existing water quality, to deliver existing levels of service and to meet all the new legally enforceable obligations notified to me by the Secretaries of State. They provide incentives for companies to use their management skills to improve performance and to cut their costs. Companies can improve discretionary services for customers out of increased efficiency.

Companies will have to invest substantially to meet their environmental obligations and face negative cash flows for a number of years. I have assumed that investment would be financed by a combination of borrowing and retained earnings. Price limits were based on low cost solutions and assumed that companies would be able to implement capital programmes within a return on capital well below that assumed by the Secretaries of State in 1989.

Reviewing the Review

The Periodic Review involved considerable resources. We have therefore reviewed the way in which we carried out the job in order to learn from our experiences and to help my successor in approaching the next Periodic Review. Both the methodology and the process we established worked well. They should be developed; but this should, in my view, be a matter of evolution and not revolution.

Chapter 6 contains the main conclusions from our review of the Review.

Sharing benefits

Utility regulation should provide incentives for companies to deliver services at lower costs. Setting limits to prices rather than to profits encourages companies to perform better. Ofwat and the quality regulators will monitor the service provided to customers and the improvements to the environment. The prime focus will be on what companies achieve, not on how much money they spend.

Customers will benefit from any savings at the next Periodic Review when price limits are reset on the basis of the costs of an efficient company. Price limits are set on the assumption that companies will be able to reduce costs in the future. If savings materialise earlier or are on a greater scale than assumed when price limits were set, I should like to see companies bring forward sharing of benefits with customers. Exactly how that might be achieved is a matter for the company. Customers would clearly like lower bills or cash refunds. They would also like better levels of service, provided that companies take full account of customers' priorities. I would like to see companies consult their Customer Service Committee about their spending plans for improved services.

Looking ahead

In the period of stability ahead, Ofwat will develop a number of important areas of regulation. In particular, a regime for monitoring outputs needs to be put in place and further progress made in relating charges to costs within the overall price limits.

Monitoring achievements

The quality regulators, the Drinking Water Inspectorate (DWI) and the National Rivers Authority (NRA) and I intend to concentrate on company performance in delivering services to customers, their progress in implementing legal requirements relating to drinking water quality and sewage treatment and their performance in dealing with growth in demand for water and sewerage services.

I will need to collect information both to monitor delivery of these outputs and ensure that companies' prices remain within the limits set. I have arranged to receive information from the NRA and the DWI on company progress in meeting their statutory quality improvements.

Ofwat will continue to collect other information on an annual basis in order to measure company performance. We will continue to publish reports which highlight and compare company financial performance, costs of water delivered and sewage collected and the level of service to customers. Where companies fall short I will ask them to report to me how they intend to improve.

The paper *Information for Regulation* (May 1995) sets all this out in detail.

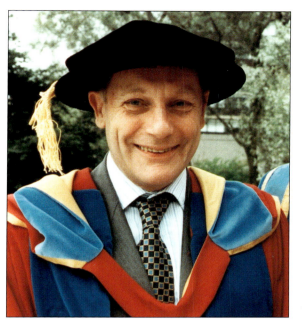

Ian Byatt receiving his honorary degree from Brunel University in July 1994 before announcing the results of the Periodic Review. Photo: courtesy of Brunel University.

Representing customers

The chairmen of the Customer Service Committees played a vital role in representing customers' interests during the Periodic Review. Ofwat's National Customer Council will develop further its role in representing customers and assist me in discharging my statutory duty to protect the interests of customers.

Important developments in customer service during the year included the development with the water industry associations of a framework of principles on compensation for poor service; a review of the way in which company complaint procedures have been operating in practice; further pressure on companies to improve their optional metering schemes - which has resulted in significant changes by some companies; and continued pressure on companies to improve their policies and procedures for handling customers in debt - which has resulted in a further fall in the number of customers disconnected.

Charges for measured and unmeasured supplies

Discriminatory charges levied on customers taking a measured supply have been significantly reduced. Increases in measured charges have been below the rate of inflation. For most companies tariff rebalancing is largely complete. But standing charges are still too high. In some cases there should be rebalancing between charges for water and sewerage services, particularly where these services are provided by separate companies within a region. On the waste water side, I want to see a better distinction between charges for domestic sewage and for trade effluent. Despite practical problems, charges for foul sewage should also be distinguished from those for surface drainage and those for highway drainage.

Large user tariffs and competition

The Competition and Service (Utilities) Act 1992 extended the provisions for direct competition to allow inset appointments to be granted for customers using over 250 megalitres of water a year. The threat of losing large industrial customers has prompted companies to think about their cost structures. In 1995-96, 18 companies have introduced tariffs for large users.

The introduction of these tariffs has been accompanied by some rebalancing of charges. Historically, there has been cross subsidisation; tariffs for some large users were higher than justified by the costs imposed on the system. As the number of customers who will be eligible for these tariffs is generally small there have only been small changes in other customers' bills.

Unit charges should not be lower for business customers merely because they use a large amount of water. To ensure that large user tariffs are not simply a response to commercial pressure, companies have been asked to provide a cost breakdown.

Charges may differ for services provided in different ways: for bulk, or - by analogy - wholesale supplies to large customers, where the distribution of water within the site is in the hands of the purchaser; and retail supplies to smaller customers.

Questions of competition also arise outside the tariff basket. Connections to a company main, where I have powers in relation to disputes about charges, is an obvious example where there is evidence of overcharging. Charges for installing optional meters also remain too high in some cases. These are both areas where I would like to see more competition. It is not essential that the water company carries out such work.

Ensuring proper ring-fencing of companies

The 1992 Competition and Service (Utilities) Act specifies that transactions between the appointed water business and all other activities of the group should be at arm's length. In March 1994 Ofwat issued guidelines to the companies on transfer pricing (ie the prices paid by the appointed business to the non-appointed business and associates for the allocation of common costs). Companies are required to certify annually to me that they comply with the guidelines. In addition, I am instigating a programme of checks. They will begin in the autumn of 1995 and will involve visits to most companies over the next two years.

Methods of charging for water

I welcomed the announcement made by the Secretary of State on 4 April 1995 that in the long term metering should be the normal basis for paying for water.

Because metering can only spread gradually, it is sensible to continue to use rateable value based charging after the year 2000. As many people are unhappy about water bills which are linked to the rateable value of their house rather than the amount of water they use, I will continue to place pressure on companies to improve their arrangements for enabling customers to exercise their right to pay by meter. Some companies still overcharge for installing optional meters; some place unreasonable restrictions on customers. They must be more accommodating.

Proposals for revised Directives in relation to both drinking water quality and sewage treatment raise the spectre of potential further price increases for customers. Ofwat will continue to raise public awareness about the scale and cost of new Directives and their possible impact on customers' bills.

The Environment Bill requires the new Environment Agency to consider the costs and benefits of assessments it sends to Ministers. It also requires the Agency to take into account costs and benefits in the carrying out of its duties. I hope that Parliament will enact these clauses.

The costs of meeting environmental obligations

In my view, it is important that the Environment Bill should place a duty on water companies to promote water conservation and the efficient use of water by their customers. I believe the Bill should give me powers to set standards of performance, for example, for meter option schemes.

I am also convinced of the desirability of a clause in the Bill which would place a statutory duty on the ten sewerage companies to promote the efficient use of sewerage services. This would save costs and facilitate integrated pollution control.

Promoting efficiency

In March 1995 Lyonnaise des Eaux, who also owns North East Water and Essex and Suffolk Water, proposed the acquisition of Northumbrian Water. The market competition aspects will be considered by the Commission of the European Communities and the comparative competition aspects by the MMC.

In my evidence to the MMC I argued that the merger would be against the public interest as it would impair my ability to carry out my statutory functions by reducing the number of comparators. Such a loss could only be remedied if the acquiring company were to make undertakings, which could be given regulatory effect, to provide specific benefits to customers, in particular lower prices.

Mergers and acquisitions

CHAPTER 2 CHAPTER

The Customer Service Committees and the Ofwat National Customer Council are at the heart of Ofwat; they represent the interests of water customers and work closely with the Director General whose statutory duties include protecting the interests of customers.

Ofwat structure

In setting up the regulatory regime for the water industry in 1989, Parliament decided that the Customer Service Committees (CSCs), which have the statutory duty to represent the interests of customers, should be established and maintained by the Director General.

The close working relations that exist between the Director General, the Ofwat National Customer Council (ONCC) and the ten regional Ofwat CSCs are a strength of the Ofwat structure which integrates customer representation with regulation.

The ten CSCs were set up just over five years ago in April 1990 by the Director General. They have statutory duties to represent the interests of customers and to investigate complaints from customers about their water and sewerage company. The ten CSC chairmen and the Director General have always met regularly; first as the CSC Chairmen's Group and, since March 1993, as the Ofwat National Customer Council.

Ian Byatt with the Ofwat National Customer Council

ONCC provides a focus for the representation of customers' interests at the national level. ONCC and the CSCs are concerned solely with the interests of customers and do not share the wider duties of the Director General. Against this background of different statutory duties and objectives, the integrated Ofwat structure ensures that there is close and regular contact between the regulator and customer representatives. The regulator benefits from informed debate before he takes his decisions and customer representatives have more power to influence those decisions. The CSCs and ONCC have overlapping duties; the interdependence that co-exists within the structure means that Ofwat is more effective in regulating the water industry and in protecting the interests of customers.

The Director General intends increasingly to use the Council as a major instrument in carrying out his statutory duty to protect the interests of water customers. This builds on the successful innovation during the 1994 Review of price limits when customer representatives were involved by the Director General in a way that was unprecedented in utility regulation. CSC chairmen had full access to confidential material and internal papers and were able to advise the Director General from a position of knowledge. (See ONCC Annual Report for a fuller account of the involvement of CSC chairmen in the Review of price limits).

The Ofwat structure will continue to rely on good communications between the Director General and his staff and the customer representatives appointed by him. Instead of unproductive confrontation, the structure produces steady progress in the regulation of the water industry and customer protection. This is as a result of the Director General, ONCC and the CSCs

- consulting and keeping each other informed about policy initiatives and developments;

- understanding each other's position and discussing differences;

- working together towards common objectives.

Details of Ofwat's achievements for customers are set out in this report and in the separately published annual reports of ONCC and the ten CSCs.

CSC membership

The Director General will maintain streamlined and effective CSCs with members and chairmen drawn from a wide range of backgrounds who bring different experience and expertise. There will be a balance between continuity of membership and some turnover in order to give new people the opportunity to serve on the CSCs. This turnover is achieved through natural wastage, ie by the retirement of members at the end of their term of office and by the occasional resignation of members for personal reasons during their term of office. In the last five years the Director General has only once terminated an appointment during a member's term of office. That was due to prolonged non-attendance at CSC meetings without reason.

Chairmen

The chairmen of the nine CSCs in England are appointed by the Director General in consultation with the President of the Board of Trade. The Chairman for the CSC for Wales is appointed in consultation with the Secretary of State for Wales.

There were no changes to chairmen during the year. However, in January 1995 the Chairman of Wessex CSC, Anthony Clothier, who was one of the inaugural

CSC chairmen, announced that he would be retiring in the Summer due to pressure from his other commitments.

Of the ten CSC chairmen, six have been in post for five years, two for two years and two for one year; three are women and seven are men.

Members

The Director General appoints all CSC members in consultation with each CSC chairman. There is a rolling programme of appointments so that the appointment of around one third of the membership falls due for review each April.

At the April 1994 review 34 members were reappointed and ten new members appointed.

Over the last five years CSC membership has grown by 17 to 120.

Members 1.4.90	Retirements	Resignations	New Appointments	Members 31.3.95
103	21	29	67	120*

* includes 73 of the original members appointed in 1990

TABLE 1 CSC MEMBERS AGE PROFILE

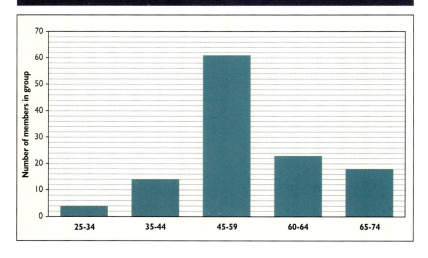

CSC members are drawn from all age groups. (See Table 1).

Of the current membership of 120, 47 are women (37 per cent). The Cabinet Office survey of public appointments (published in *Public Bodies* 1994) shows that among government departments, Ofwat has the fourth highest proportion of women appointees.

Currently four (3 per cent) of members are from ethnic minority groups and of these two are women.

The CSCs exist to represent the interests of all customers, both household and business. Currently around 32 per cent of the total CSC membership have a business background.

Recruiting members

Ofwat's recruitment procedures for CSC chairmen and members follow best practice as set out in the Cabinet Office *Guide on Public Appointments Procedures*. A full explanation is available on request.

An Ofwat information booklet *A Water Watchdog Role for You?* and an application form for those wishing to become a CSC member are available. The booklet is also produced in a large print edition and on audio cassette.

Ofwat seeks applications from all sections of the community. This helps the Director General to ensure that each Committee has members with a wide range of expertise and backgrounds. Approaches to seek nominations for membership are made regularly to consumer organisations, welfare groups, professional bodies and other groups as well as to the Cabinet Office Public Appointments Unit. Over the last year particular effort has been made to attract people with special skills relevant to regulation such as accountants, as well as those with customer service and consumer affairs experience. An article published in the Association of Accounting Technicians magazine attracted a healthy response from people interested in serving on a CSC.

The Director General with Chairman and members of Yorkshire Customer Service Committee

During the year Ofwat advertised for the first time for chairmen and members in the national and regional press. Advertisements for CSC members were placed in regional newspapers in Yorkshire, the North East, South West, East Anglia and the East End of London. The results were very encouraging and a number of people came forward who had never before considered public service.

In February an advertisement was placed in The Times and The Observer inviting applications for appointment as Wessex CSC Chairman. Fifty-four enquiries and 25 completed applications were received.

During the year Ofwat co-operated with the Women's National Commission in producing a new publication *A Woman's Guide to Public Appointments.* This contains information on the role of CSC members and features Mrs Josephine Turnbull, a member of Northumbria CSC.

The appointment of all chairmen and members is announced by means of a press release. The names of chairmen and members are also published in this Annual Report and in each CSC's Annual Report.

Nolan Committee on standards in public life

In February the Nolan Committee received evidence from the Cabinet Office Public Appointments Unit recommending improvements to public appointments procedures. Ofwat's procedures already comply with most of the recommendations made, including greater use of advertising of posts and the announcement of appointments. Ofwat does not, at present, seek references on candidates but is considering the need to do so within the context of its other procedures for the screening of candidates. These include the interview of all short listed candidates before a final decision is taken on appointment.

Members' training

Members are encouraged to attend conferences and seminars to broaden their knowledge of the water industry and its regulation. Ofwat's own three day industry course, developed with Water Training International, will, in the year ahead, be opened up to CSC members who wish to gain a comprehensive appreciation of the industry they are helping to regulate. These initiatives will enable CSC members to make a more effective contribution to customer protection.

During the year Ofwat commissioned an independent consultant to write a layman's guide on understanding company finances, pitched at the needs of CSC members and supported by a workshop. Workshops have been held for four CSCs during the year and greatly appreciated by members. Workshops for other CSCs will take place during the year ahead.

Training is being developed to improve the quality and consistency of CSC audits of company practices. Regular random audits of files at company offices by CSC members will play an increasingly important role in monitoring whether the companies are following their own published procedures or Ofwat guidelines in providing services to customers.

Members' handbook

In response to requests from CSC members, a members' handbook was produced by Ofwat and issued to all members in February. The handbook brings together in a single volume a wide range of information about the regulatory regime for the water industry, about Ofwat, the conduct of CSC business, the role of CSC members and their terms and conditions of service. The handbook is aimed primarily at meeting the needs of new and recently appointed members but is also a useful source of reference for longer serving members. Members like it.

Honours

In the 1995 New Years Honours list Janet Graham a former member of Southern CSC was awarded the MBE. This was the first time that a CSC member had received an honour for work on behalf of consumers as a CSC member.

In the same Honours list Jim Gardner, Chairman of the Ofwat National Customer Council and of Northumbria CSC was awarded the CVO for services as Chairman of the Trustees of the Prince's Trust.

The effectiveness of Ofwat's integrated structure depends on maintaining good two way communications between Headquarters in Birmingham and the ten CSC offices. Details of the principal means of communication were set out in the 1993 Annual Report.

During the Periodic Review CSCs continued to deal with customers' complaints and the research, development and implementation of improvements in company policies carried on largely unaffected. Headquarters staff, despite the priority given to Periodic Review related work, continued to provide the CSCs with the essential support they needed.

In addition to regular contact between the Director General and CSC chairmen, inside as well as outside the Ofwat National Customer Council, the Director General or his deputy regularly attended meetings of CSC regional managers during the Periodic Review to keep them fully up to date with Ofwat's work and to answer questions. During the year some regional managers' meetings were held away from Birmingham in CSC offices. This has improved the exchange of information and ideas between CSCs and has brought regional managers and individual CSC chairmen together for discussions.

Communication with the CSCs

Because of the Periodic Review the Director General was represented by his deputy at the annual meetings with CSCs in 1994. These meetings were primarily used to brief the CSCs on the progress of the Periodic Review and to give members the opportunity to feed their views directly into the process before the Director General issued draft determinations of the new price limits to the companies. The Deputy Director General also answered a wide range of non-Periodic Review questions from CSC members during his meetings with the CSCs.

During 1995 the Director General will again be visiting all the CSCs for discussions with members. These visits demonstrate the value that is placed on the contribution of the CSCs to Ofwat's work.

Annual visits to CSCs

There was no conference in 1994 because of the Periodic Review. The next conference is on 8 and 9 November 1995 and will again be held under the auspices of ONCC. Planning and organisation of the conference started in the New Year and is the responsibility of an ONCC working group, which includes eight CSC members and is supported by Ofwat staff. The Director General and senior Ofwat staff will attend the conference.

Members' conference

CSC staff

Each CSC is typically supported by a full-time secretariat comprising a regional manager/committee secretary, two assistant managers and clerical and secretarial staff. At 31 March 1995 there were 48 permanent full time staff in the CSC secretariats.

CSC staff are appointed by the Director General but are officers and employees of the CSCs *not* of the Director General. In practice CSC staff are appointed on the recommendation of the CSC Chairman. Vacancies are normally advertised in the regional press as well as within Ofwat. During the year new regional managers were appointed to Northumbria, Southern, South West and Thames CSCs.

Security of staff

The CSCs provide a service to the public and offices are open to personal visitors (preferably by appointment). CSC staff also visit customers at home when circumstances require it.

Staff are very occasionally exposed to abusive and threatening behaviour from customers which causes them to fear for their personal safety. All CSCs follow a Code of Practice on security to minimise the risk and to ensure that, as far as possible, the safety and protection of staff both on the CSC premises and when making visits to customers is paramount. In addition, works have been carried out at all CSC offices to improve their security.

Happily most members of the public appreciate the quality of service provided by CSC staff even if the answer to their particular enquiry or complaint is not the one they were hoping for.

Standards of service

Standards of service for complaint handling by the CSCs and for the conduct of other business by the CSCs were brought into operation in 1993-94. The standards were agreed between the Director General and the ten CSC chairmen.

The national results for 1994-95 and the previous year are shown in Table 2.

TABLE 2 CSC STANDARDS OF SERVICE

Service standard	Achievement 1993-94	Achievement 1994-95
CSC offices to be continuously staffed between published hours on normal working days.	100% compliance, except for unavoidable closures due to staff absence on duties elsewhere.	100% compliance, except for unavoidable closures due to staff absence on duties elsewhere.
Outside of office hours (and when unavoidably the office is not attended during office hours) an answering machine to be in operation.	100% compliance.	100% compliance.
Calls left on answering machines to be returned where required within two hours of the office re-opening.	98.8% compliance.	99.8% compliance.
Customer enquiries (written and telephone) to be answered within two working days with a target of 95%.	99.9% compliance.	99.9% compliance.
Agenda and papers for CSC meetings to be despatched at least five working days before meetings.	100% compliance.	100% compliance.
Draft minutes of CSC meetings to be circulated within 10 working days.	91% compliance.	98% compliance.
Complaints to be actioned within five working days of receipt with a target of 95%.	98.5% compliance.	98.3% compliance.
Complaints to be cleared up within 40 working days of receipt with a target of 80%.	83.7% compliance.	88.1% compliance.

CUSTOMER COMPLAINTS, DISPUTES AND APPEALS

Customers need effective complaint handling procedures to resolve their problems. They should receive compensation when they receive a sub-standard service. The year has seen progress in both these areas which will help to ensure that customer interests are properly protected.

The revised Guaranteed Standards Scheme

Figures relating to the revised and improved Guaranteed Standards Scheme (GSS) became available during the year. The GSS lays down standards of service that must be met by companies in every case; if the company fails to meet the standard it must make a compensatory payment to the customer affected. Most of the standards set in 1989 were improved and a number of new ones were introduced with effect from 1 April 1993. The amount of compensation payable was increased from £5 to £10 with rebates of charges for sewer flooding up to a limit of £1,000.

During 1992-93 1,760 claims were made and 1,917 payments made. In 1993-94, the first year of the revised scheme, the number of payments increased significantly to 11,388. The total value of the payments made was £214,101 compared with £9,585 in the previous year. Ofwat will continue to keep the GSS under review to see where improvements may be made.

Company complaints procedures

The Competition and Service (Utilities) Act 1992 required water and sewerage companies to have their complaints procedures approved by the Director General.

Ofwat only approved those complaints procedures which were likely to be effective in providing customers with proper outcomes to their complaints with readily accessible and well signposted avenues for complaint and good complaint handling procedures. Ofwat is working to ensure that customers in different parts of the country should receive consistent standards of complaint handling. In the long term improved procedures should reduce the need for Ofwat to investigate complaints and should lead to a reduction in the number of complaints it receives.

Since approval of company complaints procedures in 1993, CSCs have monitored their implementation. As part of this process Ofwat conducted a survey involving over 600 complaints handled by CSCs in the first three months of 1994-95. Each CSC provided a report to the Director General setting out its views on individual company procedure.

The findings of the survey, and the views reported by CSCs will be published in the summer of 1995. The ability to make comparisons between companies has been critical in monitoring how individual companies apply their policies in practice. In most cases companies' complaints procedures have improved and many companies are more ready to make compensation payments in appropriate cases. Ofwat has already begun to see a reduction in the number of complaints received. Some companies, however, still have a long way to go before they have effective complaints procedures.

Ofwat's report will indicate which companies are regarded as having better complaint handling practices than others and signpost ways in which other companies should be improving their procedures.

South West CSC meeting customers at the Regulators' Roadshow

By its very nature the GSS scheme must be simple to operate with clear and precise standards. This means that there are many situations where things have gone wrong in the delivery of services that are not covered in the GSS; in particular it cannot cover important aspects of service such as supply problems due to inadequate water pressure or the taste and appearance of tap water.

In many cases resolution of customer complaints about poor service includes financial redress, either in the form of compensation or a refund of charges paid.

Ofwat has been working with the industry to agree a framework of principles on compensation to ensure that all companies adopt a consistent approach to the issue of financial redress for substandard service. The Water Services Association (WSA) and Water Companies Association (WCA) have now agreed that the starting principle is that if goods or services, for which customers are paying, are not suitable for the purpose or are of a poor standard which causes demonstrable loss or inconvenience to customers, the customer should receive compensation. This is not a new principle but the CSCs report that it is one that some companies do not always follow.

CSCs will be discussing compensation in more detail with each of the companies during 1995. As a result of the framework of principles, the Director General expects CSCs to report fewer complaints about companies' refusal to pay compensation in recognition of poor service.

Compensation for poor service

Ofwat's complaints procedure

Ofwat provides an independent complaint handling service for customers who are dissatisfied with the answer they have received from their water and sewerage company. Ofwat will not normally take up a complaint until the company's complaints procedure, approved by the Director General, has been exhausted and the customer remains dissatisfied.

During the year Ofwat published its own complaints procedure. This contains detailed advice to customers on how to make complaints to Ofwat and the principles and procedures that are applied in investigating and resolving them.

The ten CSCs have the statutory duty to investigate complaints; they deal with most of the complaints received by Ofwat. The Director General has a statutory responsibility for dealing with certain complaints. He also has powers to determine some types of dispute and his decision is binding on both the company and the customer.

A CSC must refer a complaint which it has been unable to resolve to the Director General for him to consider. The Director General is also responsible for dealing with complaints that a CSC has failed to carry out its complaint investigation duties properly. If customers are unhappy with the way that the Director General has dealt with their complaints the matter may be referred via the customer's MP to the Parliamentary Ombudsman.

Ofwat's complaints procedure contains information and advice on all of these matters as well as explaining which complaints fall outside Ofwat's statutory duties and are the responsibility of the NRA or of other bodies. In addition to the main document there is a summary leaflet which has been awarded the Crystal Mark by the Plain English Campaign.

Complaints management

The complaints procedure is supported by Ofwat's internal complaints manual. The manual was completely revised during the year in the light of experience of complaint handling over the past five years. It contains detailed guidance on complaint handling procedures designed to ensure that customers' complaints are dealt with quickly, efficiently and consistently throughout Ofwat. The manual also contains policy and precedent advice which is regularly updated.

A working group comprising complaint handling staff from the CSCs and Headquarters has met during the year to identify ways of further improving the quality and efficiency of complaint handling by Ofwat. The group played a major role in the revision of the complaints manual.

As part of a wider review of Ofwat information systems, work started on a review of Ofwat's complaint database and management system, Watercare. The aim is to

TABLE 3 CSCS: NUMBER OF COMPLAINTS RECEIVED BY COMPANY

Company	Number of connections to the nearest 1,000 1994-95	Number of complaints received 1994-95	Rate per 10,000 connections 1994-95	Number of complaints received 1993-94	Rate per 10,000 connections 1993-94
Water and sewerage companies					
Anglian Water Services Ltd.	2,337,000	1,055	4.5	921	4.0
Dŵr Cymru Cyfyngedig	1,295,000	1,175	9.1	1,248	9.9
North West Water Ltd.	2,912,000	801	2.8	885	3.1
Northumbrian Water Ltd.	1,159,000	218	1.9	279	2.4
Severn Trent Water Ltd.	3,556,000	1,178	3.3	1,135	3.2
South West Water Services Ltd.	654,000	701	10.7	1,148	17.1
Southern Water Services Ltd.	1,689,000	487	2.9	699	4.2
Thames Water Utilities Ltd.	5,012,000	3,748	7.5	3,168	6.4
Wessex Water Services Ltd.	1,026,000	411	4.0	532	5.2
Yorkshire Water Services Ltd.	2,010,000	1,121	5.6	1,910	9.5
Water only companies					
Bournemouth & West Hampshire Water Companies	175,000	84	4.8	71	4.0
Bristol Water plc	430,000	185	4.3	246	5.7
Cambridge Water Company	110,000	69	6.3	61	5.6
Chester Waterworks Company	45,000	22	4.9	11	2.5
Cholderton & District Water Company Ltd.	1,000	2	*	0	*
East Surrey Water plc	133,000	113	8.5	103	7.7
Essex & Suffolk Water plc	685,000	255	3.7	358	5.1
Folkestone & Dover Water Services Ltd.	66,000	40	6.1	31	4.5
Hartlepool Water plc	38,000	11	2.9	14	3.7
Mid Kent Water plc	216,000	254	11.8	142	6.7
Mid Southern Water plc	271,000	150	5.5	112	4.2
North East Water plc	563,000	229	4.1	281	5.0
North Surrey Water Ltd.	194,000	112	5.8	42	2.2
Portsmouth Water plc	270,000	100	3.7	62	2.2
South East Water Ltd.	260,000	159	6.1	281	10.4
South Staffordshire Water plc	506,000	118	2.3	195	3.9
Sutton District Water plc	118,000	41	3.5	41	3.5
Tendring Hundred Water Services Ltd.	63,000	46	7.3	53	8.4
Three Valleys Water Services plc	956,000	385	4.0	209	2.2
Wrexham & East Denbighshire Water Company	61,000	31	5.1	31	5.1
York Waterworks plc	74,000	9	1.2	26	3.5
National total	**26,884,000**	**13,310**	**5.0**	**14,295**	**5.4**

Notes

The number of connections has been taken from the additional information supplied with each company's Principal Statement for 1995-96. For the water and sewerage companies the figure is the total number of properties connected for both water and sewerage plus the number connected for water only and the number for sewerage only.

* Cholderton is an exceptionally small company.

upgrade it to meet Ofwat's developing data requirements for monitoring the performance of companies in the second quinquennium of the regulatory regime. It will also provide a more efficient complaint management system for the benefit of complaint handling staff and customers alike.

CSC complaints

The number of complaints received by the CSCs in 1994-95 was 13,310 nearly 7 per cent down on the previous year. This was the second consecutive year that the number of complaints had fallen since the peak of 14,792 in 1992-93.

This year, for the first time, complaints received by the CSCs have been classified according to whether the customer made any use of the company's complaints

TABLE 4 CSCS: NUMBER OF COMPLAINTS RECEIVED BY MONTH

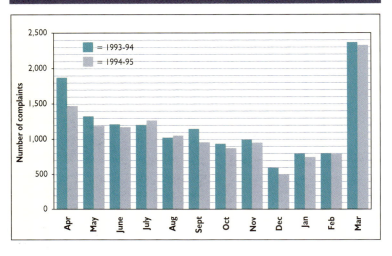

TABLE 5 CSCS: COMPLAINTS BY CATEGORY

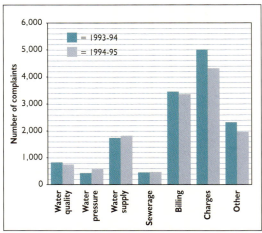

TABLE 6 CSCS: TRENDS IN COMPLAINT NUMBERS (12 MONTH MOVING AVERAGE)

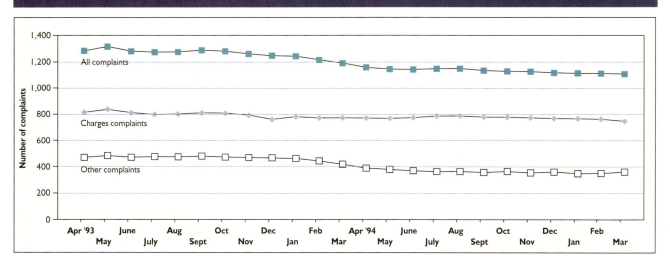

procedure and whether that procedure had been fully exhausted. Thirty-four per cent of customers who complained to the CSCs during 1994-95 had not previously approached the company about their complaint while 56 per cent of customers referred their complaint to the CSC before the company's complaint procedure had been exhausted. Only 10 per cent of complaints received by the CSCs came from customers who had followed the company complaints procedure through to the end.

The development of company complaint procedures has meant that the proportion of complaints received by the CSCs that are then referred back to and resolved by the companies rose from 44 per cent in 1993-94 to 52 per cent in 1994-95. The proportion of complaints received that were investigated and resolved by the CSCs fell from 53 per cent in 1993-94 to 44 per cent in 1994-95. As a result of the development of more effective complaint procedures by the water industry the CSCs seem now to be dealing with the more difficult and intractable cases while the more straightforward complaints are being dealt with by companies.

In 12 per cent of cases CSCs secured compensation or rebates for customers as part of a resolution of the complaint. The total amount in compensation and rebates reported by the ten CSCs in 1994-95 was £584,485. This brings the total for the last four years to £3.25 million. Where compensation for poor service or a rebate form an appropriate element in resolving a complaint, the companies are expected increasingly to make payments to customers without the necessity for CSC intervention. CSCs will also look to companies to tackle the underlying causes of customer dissatisfaction which generate complaints and to improve services in these areas.

Complaints received against water companies are sorted into one or more of over 100 sub-categories. For this report, complaints have been grouped into seven main categories, both nationally and for each of the ten CSC regions (see Table 7 and 8). Nationally the proportion of complaints received under each category has remained broadly in line with 1993-94. Complaints peaked in February, March and April coinciding with the annual billing cycle.

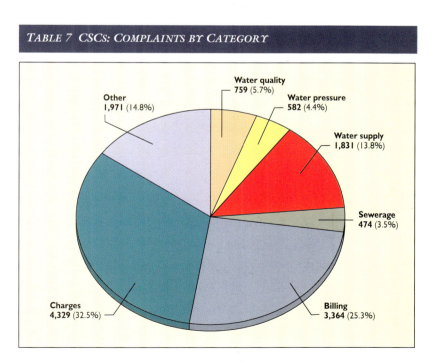

TABLE 7 CSCs: COMPLAINTS BY CATEGORY

Water quality 759 (5.7%)
Water pressure 582 (4.4%)
Water supply 1,831 (13.8%)
Sewerage 474 (3.5%)
Billing 3,364 (25.3%)
Charges 4,329 (32.5%)
Other 1,971 (14.8%)

TABLE 8 CSCs: COMPLAINTS BY CATEGORY

CSC	Water quality No.	%	Water pressure No.	%	Water supply No.	%	Sewerage No.	%	Billing No.	%	Charges No.	%	Other No.	%
Central	64	5.0	60	4.6	249	19.2	48	3.7	354	27.3	400	30.9	121	9.3
Eastern	52	3.7	29	2.0	93	6.5	47	3.3	264	18.5	724	50.8	216	15.2
North West	64	8.0	57	7.1	120	15.0	43	5.4	177	22.1	241	30.1	99	12.3
Nothumbria	87	19.0	32	7.0	75	16.4	18	3.9	95	20.8	122	26.6	29.0	6.3
South West	48	6.9	14	2.0	36	5.1	18	2.6	151	21.5	365	52.1	69	9.8
Southern	42	4.0	18	1.7	89	8.6	72	6.9	293	28.2	350	33.7	176	16.9
Thames	111	2.4	213	4.7	685	15.1	133	2.9	1,312	28.8	1,176	25.9	919	20.2
Wales	146	11.9	62	5.0	140	11.4	34	2.8	348	28.3	324	26.4	174	14.2
Wessex	31	4.5	10	1.5	59	8.7	19	2.8	159	23.3	333	48.8	71	10.4
Yorkshire	114	10.1	87	7.7	285	25.2	42	3.7	211	18.7	294	26.0	97	8.6
National total	**759**	**5.7**	**582**	**4.4**	**1,831**	**13.8**	**474**	**3.5**	**3,364**	**25.3**	**4,329**	**32.5**	**1,971**	**14.8**

Despite the announcement last July by the Director General of new lower price limits, customers remain concerned about their water bills. The level and increases in charges, tariff structures and rebalancing and charging methods are the main areas of concern. Companies tend to tell customers that Ofwat is responsible for the size of their bill rather than taking responsibility for explaining properly to their customers that their charges are within the price limits determined by the Director General and accepted by the companies.

TABLE 9 CSCs: COMPLAINTS BY CUSTOMER TYPE

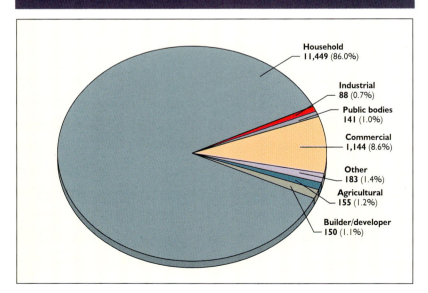

- Household 11,449 (86.0%)
- Industrial 88 (0.7%)
- Public bodies 141 (1.0%)
- Commercial 1,144 (8.6%)
- Other 183 (1.4%)
- Agricultural 155 (1.2%)
- Builder/developer 150 (1.1%)

Overall, complaints about charges fell to 32.5 per cent, nearly 3 per cent down on the previous year. At the regional level, Eastern, South West and Wessex CSCs received the largest proportion of complaints about charges.

The proportion of complaints received about water quality matters in the Northumbria CSC region remained at about three times the national level. Water quality complaints in Yorkshire and Wales were also well above the national average, while Thames CSC again recorded the lowest proportion of such complaints (just over 2 per cent).

There were also wide variations in the proportion of complaints received about water supply matters (which include connections and interruptions to supply) with the proportion received by the Yorkshire CSC running at nearly twice the national figure. Complaints to Central CSC increased substantially because of a hosepipe ban imposed by Severn Trent.

The proportion of complaints in the 'other' category (which includes problems with company administration) rose sharply in Southern CSC's region to nearly 17 per cent compared with 5 per cent the year before. In contrast, the proportion of complaints received by Thames CSC fell from 27 per cent to 20 per cent, reflecting a reduction in complaints about company administration.

To monitor the quality of Ofwat's complaint handling procedures, customers are sent a short questionnaire (with return postage pre-paid), after each complaint has been dealt with. Since the customer satisfaction survey started in April 1993 the response rate has been consistently higher than 50 per cent and is well above that originally anticipated for such a survey.

The results for this year and last year are summarised in Table 10.

Information from the survey helps to improve complaint handling. The results of the survey are circulated to CSCs quarterly. In addition, all questionnaires containing significant comments are passed back to the CSC office to complete the cycle.

Survey of customers' satisfaction with complaint handling

TABLE 10 CUSTOMER SATISFACTION SURVEY SUMMARY

		1993* %	1994** %
Response rate		58	57
Outcome of complaint	Resolved the matter	24	23
	Partly resolved the matter	18	20
	Did not resolve the matter	58	57
Speed of response	More quickly than expected	33	34
	As quickly as expected	51	51
	Less quickly than expected	16	15
Quality of service	Good	24	45
	Satisfactory	18	24
	Poor	58	31

* Refers to the period 1 April 1993 to 31 December 1993
** Refers to the period 1 January 1994 to 31 December 1994

Customers' comments range from the unprintable to the very appreciative and humorous. Of the (printable) critical comments:

- "I've done more work for you by completing this survey, than you have done for me."

- "You seem to believe all that the water companies say, but all their lies are not true."

- "Your comments were as much use as an ashtray on a motorbike or a bull's udder." But:

- "What I tried doing for months with [water company] you did in one day. Thank you."

- "Without Ofwat I don't think that the matter would have been resolved before Christmas."

- "The person I spoke to went to great lengths to explain the reasons for price increases and how Ofwat worked in the interest of the customers."

And in the humorous category:

- "You handled the complaint very well. But the only difference between Dick Turpin and the water companies is that Dick Turpin had the decency to wear a mask when he robbed people."

TABLE 11 COMPLAINTS DEALT WITH/STATE OF PLAY

	1993 – 1994		1994 – 1995	
Brought forward from previous year	3,050		2,900	
Received	14,295		13,310	
Closed:	Number	%	Number	%
Accepted for investigation and resolved a)	7,691	53	6,043	44
Referred to company and resolved b)	6,318	44	7,076	52
Withdrawn/not pursued by customer c)	267	2	161	1
Outside jurisdiction	168	1	391	3
Unresolved d)	1	0	3	0
Total	14,445	100	13,674	100
	14,445		13,674	
Carried forward to following year	2,900		2,536	

Notes
a) Complaints received which the company has generally had an opportunity to deal with but the customer remained dissatisfied.
b) Complaints received which had not exhausted the company's complaints procedure.
c) Complaints received mostly by telephone and not followed up in writing where the customer agreed to do so.
d) Complaints considered by the Director General, after referral to him by the CSC, where he was unable to secure a satisfactory resolution.

The operation of the Customer Satisfaction Survey was reviewed during the year. As a result, an amended questionnaire was introduced from April 1995 which invites customers to give their name and address so that Ofwat can follow up comments about the handling of individual complaints. At present the survey is run in-house, but Ofwat is looking into the possibility of contracting out aspects of its operation.

Complaints considered by the Director General

A total of 116 complaints were received by the Director General in 1994-95. Apart from complaints against CSCs, issues raised included fairness of tariffs, breaches by companies of statutory duties in respect of service quality, and the application of infrastructure charges.

CSCs referred 12 cases to the Director General where they had been unable to resolve the complaint with the company. The Director General supported the CSC's recommendation in six cases, as a result of which complainants received rebates or compensation amounting to over £35,000. Cases successfully resolved included one in which Yorkshire Water paid £3,000 towards the costs of a local gala following regular discolouration of the water supply in the locality; and North West Water agreed to rebate a proportion of the bills of three customers who had suffered low pressure over a period of two years.

The Director General must consider complaints alleging that CSCs have not investigated customers' complaints properly. Thirty-eight such complaints were considered. Thirty-one were not upheld. One was referred back to the CSC for further investigation. In six cases the Director concluded that the CSC should have acted differently and, following further investigation, remedies were secured for the customers concerned.

TABLE 11 CSCs: COMPLAINTS BY REFERRAL TYPE 1994-95

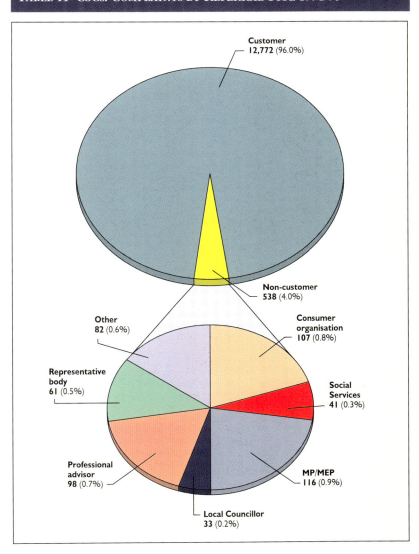

Customer
12,772 (96.0%)

Non-customer
538 (4.0%)

Consumer organisation
107 (0.8%)

Social Services
41 (0.3%)

MP/MEP
116 (0.9%)

Local Councillor
33 (0.2%)

Professional advisor
98 (0.7%)

Representative body
61 (0.5%)

Other
82 (0.6%)

In total, rebates or compensation amounting to £62,344 were obtained for customers in respect of complaints dealt with by the Director General.

Connection charges

In September 1992 the Director General was given the power to settle disputes about connections to the mains for the supply of water for domestic purposes. The Director General has determined 28 disputes to date. In 23 cases the determination was in favour of the customer.

A variety of connection works including short single standard connections, multiple connections and non-standard connections have been the subject of dispute. Where the determinations were in favour of the customer, the refunds which the companies were required to make ranged from £25 to £2,873 against charges ranging from £220 to £4,778.

When settling disputes the Director General considers four components - connection work, materials, reinstatement and overheads - the combined costs of which amount to the total charge.

In respect of connection and reinstatement work it is generally assumed that if a contractor is engaged following a competition, the contractor's rate is reasonable. When in-house labour is used, which it has been in most cases, the direct labour costs are compared with the costs which would have been incurred had the work been contracted out. That is, they are compared with market rates.

Both the company and the person requesting the connection are invited to submit information about the work involved and comment upon information provided by each other before a final determination is made.

Mike Saunders, Head of Consumer Affairs with Mike Hegarty, Operations Manager at East Surrey Water.
Photo: courtesy of East Surrey Water.

The largest refunds, when expressed as a percentage of the charge, have tended to be for large meter or multiple connections where the charges were based on an estimate of the costs rather than actual costs.

The Director General considers that this work should be opened up to competition.

Sewer adoption appeals

The Competition and Service (Utilities) Act 1992 gave the Director General the responsibility for considering appeals about the adoption of sewers. The first of these appeals was made during the year. One such appeal was by a developer wishing to enter into a Section 104 agreement for the adoption of a pumping station. A Section 104 agreement is an agreement whereby the sewerage undertaker agrees to adopt sewer works in advance of their construction by the developer.

This year was the first opportunity for the Director General to consider the issue and he has concluded that, generally, sewer works, including pumping stations, should be adopted provided that:

- the development, and the associated sewer works, have been planned in a way which provides for efficient drainage of the properties concerned;

- the design and standard of construction comply with the standards prevailing at the time the proposal for adoption is made. These standards are set out in *Sewers for Adoption (fourth edition)*, whose use is recommended by the WSA and House Builders Federation and supported by the Director General.

- the sewer works are in a satisfactory condition. That is, there are no outstanding maintenance problems;

- the sewer works are compatible with the company's existing sewer system so that adoption would not present operational problems for the company; and

- there is easy access to the sewers for maintenance purposes, which generally means that the sewer must be laid in the highway or land open to the public.

The principle underlying the above criteria is that adoption by the company should not impose costs on it which could have been avoided. The Director General accepts, however, that there may be circumstances when the costs associated with the sewers which are the subject of an appeal, though unavoidable and necessarily incurred in the provision of the sewerage system, are so high that it would be unreasonable for the sewerage undertaker to agree to adopt them.

CHAPTER 4 CHAPTER

PAYING FOR WATER

Progress has continued in securing a fair balance between measured and unmeasured tariffs. Standing charges have fallen. The Periodic Review has slowed down the increase in charges - some customers bills are falling in real terms. Meter option schemes continue to improve. Disconnections overall have fallen but companies could still do more to help those who have difficulty in paying their bills.

Charges for 1995-96

The price limits set by the Director General in July 1994 for the second half of the 1990s are generally lower than the price limits set by the Secretaries of State in 1989 for this period.

For 1995-96, average unmeasured household water bills have risen by 4.2 per cent and sewerage bills by 6.8 per cent including inflation. Average measured household water bills have risen by 0.4 per cent and sewerage bills by 1.5 per cent including inflation. In real terms average measured bills are falling.

Most of the increases result from the investment necessary to meet new EC requirements, which contributes to the £24 billion companies will have to spend over the next ten years. If it were not for these legally binding requirements, average water and sewerage bills would be falling in real terms.

Paying for quality

Better costing of environmental obligations was a key element of the Periodic Review. Ofwat will continue to work with the water companies and quality regulators to assess the implications for customers' bills of any proposals for new or revised EC directives.

In March 1995 the Director General presented evidence to the House of Lords Select Committee on the European Community on the proposed revisions to the Bathing Waters Directive. He expressed concern about the implications for water customers' bills of programmes of environmental improvement which tended to bring benefits to only certain sections of the public. Environmental improvement may be desirable but it must be affordable.

The proposed revisions to the Bathing Water Directive could cost some £4 billion. The potential increase in household bills is up to £28 on average for the eight companies affected and possibly double that in some companies.

Since price limits were set in July 1994, the EC has also proposed a revision to the Drinking Water Directive involving, in particular, heavy expenditure on

TABLE 12 1995-96 AVERAGE HOUSEHOLD BILLS FOR WATER [1]

Company	% increase 89-90 – 94-95		% increase 94-95 – 95-96		Level for 95-96
	Nominal [2]	Real [3]	Nominal [2]	Real [3]	£
Water and sewerage companies					
Anglian Water Services Ltd.	87.6	45.7	5.0	2.4	127
Dŵr Cymru Cyfyngedig	67.5	30.1	1.0	-1.6	130
North West Water Ltd.	66.2	29.1	6.0	3.3	91
Northumbrian Water Ltd.	68.9	31.2	7.0	4.3	94
Severn Trent Water Ltd.	73.7	35.0	2.7	0.1	84
South West Water Services Ltd.[4]	88.6	46.5	4.1	1.4	124
Southern Water Services Ltd.	64.2	27.6	8.1	5.4	90
Thames Water Utilities Ltd.	53.2	19.0	4.0	1.4	83
Wessex Water Services Ltd.	66.8	29.6	5.9	3.2	109
Yorkshire Water Services Ltd.	52.5	18.5	2.3	-0.3	99
Water only companies					
Bournemouth & West Hampshire Water Companies	75.4	36.2	1.6	-1.0	91
Bristol Water plc	55.0	20.4	5.2	2.5	97
Cambridge Water Company	79.6	39.5	1.6	-1.0	101
Chester Waterworks Company	45.3	12.9	0.6	-2.0	105
Cholderton & District Water Company Ltd.	65.2	28.3	2.6	0.0	122
East Surrey Water plc	82.6	41.9	2.0	-0.6	151
Essex & Suffolk Water plc	74.3	35.4	5.8	3.1	107
Folkestone & Dover Water Services Ltd.	91.7	48.9	3.8	1.2	112
Hartlepool Water plc	76.3	37.0	4.8	2.1	84
Mid Kent Water plc	58.5	23.2	3.5	0.9	124
Mid Southern Water plc	80.6	40.3	2.5	-0.1	112
North East Water plc	65.9	28.9	2.3	-0.3	91
North Surrey Water Ltd.	104.3	58.7	5.8	3.1	101
Portsmouth Water plc [4]	54.9	20.3	2.9	0.3	72
South East Water Ltd.	88.7	46.6	0.6	-2.0	158
South Staffordshire Water plc	55.8	21.1	-0.5	-3.1	73
Sutton District Water plc	95.5	51.9	1.9	-0.7	115
Tendring Hundred Water Services Ltd.	140.2	86.6	1.3	-1.3	143
Three Valleys Water Services plc	59.0	23.5	9.2	6.4	100
Wrexham & East Denbighshire Water Company	83.2	42.3	0.6	-2.0	130
York Waterworks plc	54.7	20.2	2.3	-0.3	84

[1] Average household bills include metered and unmeasured customers.

[2] Nominal percentage increases include the effect of inflation. Retail prices increased by 28.7 per cent between 1989-90 and 1994-95, and 2.6 per cent between 1994-95 and 1995-96.

[3] Real percentage increases exclude inflation.

[4] South West and Portsmouth information is the latest available pending the MMC decision on their price limits.

Company	% increase 89-90 – 94-95		% increase 94-95 – 95-96		Level for 95-96
	Nominal [2]	Real [3]	Nominal [2]	Real [3]	£
Water and sewerage companies					
Anglian Water Services Ltd.	50.1	16.6	6.9	4.2	148
Dŵr Cymru Cyfyngedig	76.3	36.9	5.2	2.5	133
North West Water Ltd.	63.4	26.9	7.3	4.5	104
Northumbrian Water Ltd.	80.8	40.4	5.5	2.8	105
Severn Trent Water Ltd.	66.2	29.1	6.8	4.1	105
South West Water Services Ltd.[4]	121.3	71.9	4.0	1.4	193
Southern Water Services Ltd.	58.2	22.9	6.6	3.9	124
Thames Water Utilities Ltd.	69.6	31.8	7.0	4.2	89
Wessex Water Services Ltd.	56.4	21.5	4.1	1.4	125
Yorkshire Water Services Ltd.	58.8	23.4	13.1	10.2	108

TABLE 13 1995-96 AVERAGE HOUSEHOLD BILLS FOR SEWERAGE [1]

[1] Average household bills include metered and unmeasured customers.

[2] Nominal percentage increases include the effect of inflation. Retail prices increased by 28.7 per cent between 1989-90 and 1994-95, and 2.6 per cent between 1994-95 and 1995-96.

[3] Real percentage increases exclude inflation.

[4] South West information is the latest available pending the MMC decision on their price limits.

replacing lead pipes. There are also proposals for a Directive on the ecological quality of water, the impact of which is not yet clear but the proposals could also have a significant effect on bills.

Key principles of charging policy

The principles outlined by the Director General in *Paying for Water: the way ahead* continue to guide Ofwat's approach to charging issues.

Water customers have little or no choice over their supplier. The charges they pay should, therefore, be fair between different 'classes' of customers and show no undue discrimination or preference. In order to do this, charges should broadly reflect costs for each customer group. Companies must meet this requirement under Condition E of the licence under which they operate.

Tariff rebalancing

Metered customers have not generally received a fair deal from their water companies. Metered customers have been paying more, on average, for the same water and sewerage service than their unmeasured counterparts. The Director General believes that any difference between the two bills (the differential) should be no more than the additional costs of metering. Ofwat estimates this to be no more than £26 per annum in 1995-96 prices, split on a two thirds/one third basis to give £17 for water and £9 for sewerage in 1995-96 prices.

TABLE 14 1995-96 CHARGES LIMITS AND TARIFF INCREASES

Company	K	Charges limit RPI + K + U (RPI = 2.6%)	Tariff basket increase	Difference between limit & tariff basket increase [3]
Water and sewerage companies				
Anglian Water Services Ltd.	1.5	4.1	4.1	0.0
Dŵr Cymru Cyfyngedig	0.5	3.1	2.5	0.6
North West Water Ltd.	2.5	5.1	5.1	0.1
Northumbrian Water Ltd.	2.5	5.1	4.6	0.5
Severn Trent Water Ltd.	0.5	3.1	3.1	0.0
South West Water Services Ltd.[2]	1.5	4.1	4.1	0.0
Southern Water Services Ltd.	4.0	6.6	6.6	0.0
Thames Water Utilities Ltd.	0.5	3.1	3.1	0.0
Wessex Water Services Ltd.	1.5	4.1	4.1	0.0
Yorkshire Water Services Ltd.	2.5	5.1	5.1	0.0
Water only companies				
Bournemouth & West Hampshire Water Companies	-0.5	2.1	2.1	0.0
Bristol Water plc	1.0	3.6	3.6	0.0
Cambridge Water Company	-2.0	0.6	0.6	0.1
Chester Waterworks Company [1]	-3.0	1.6	1.6	0.0
Cholderton & District Water Company Ltd. [1]	-1.7	2.6	2.6	0.0
East Surrey Water plc [1]	-3.0	1.6	1.6	0.0
Essex & Suffolk Water plc	2.0	4.6	4.6	0.0
Folkestone & Dover Water Services Ltd.	-0.5	2.1	2.1	0.0
Hartlepool Water plc	1.5	4.1	4.1	0.0
Mid Kent Water plc	1.0	3.6	3.6	0.0
Mid Southern Water plc [1]	-2.4	1.6	1.6	0.0
North East Water plc [1]	-3.5	2.6	2.6	0.0
North Surrey Water Ltd.	2.0	4.6	4.6	0.0
Portsmouth Water plc [1, 2]	-2.3	2.3	2.3	0.0
South East Water Ltd.	-1.0	1.6	1.6	0.0
South Staffordshire Water plc [1]	-4.1	2.1	-0.2	2.4
Sutton District Water plc [1]	-2.5	1.1	1.1	0.0
Tendring Hundred Water Services Ltd.	-0.5	2.1	2.1	0.0
Three Valleys Water Services plc	2.5	5.1	5.1	0.0
Wrexham & East Denbighshire Water Company	-2.0	0.6	0.6	0.0
York Waterworks plc [1]	-1.1	2.6	2.6	0.0

[1] U represents underspend in the charges limit in previous years. K + U is therefore the permitted increase in charges over and above inflation. (U is zero for all other companies).

[2] South West and Portsmouth information is the latest available pending the MMC decision on their price limits.

[3] Figures shown to one decimal place. Difference may not add due to rounding..

The Director General requested all companies to have a tariff action plan in place by September 1993 explaining how any imbalance between measured and unmeasured customers would be addressed. Most companies have now balanced their tariffs between these two groups of customers. Ofwat will press the five companies that have not yet reduced the differential to the maximum justifiable level of £26 (or below) to do so in 1996-97.

The report *1995-96 Tariff structure and charges* (May 1995) covers this subject in more detail but progress can be summarised as follows.

Tariffs for the 21 water only companies show that:

- since 1991-92 all companies have reduced the measured/unmeasured differential;

- the average differential in 1991-92 was £45, for 1995-96 it is £10;

- in 1991-92 all companies except two had differentials greater than the target;

- for 1995-96 all companies except two (South Staffordshire and Portsmouth) have differentials equal to or less than the target.

Tariffs for the ten water and sewerage companies show that:

- for all companies differentials have reduced since 1991-92;

- the average differential in 1991-92 was £62, for 1995-96 it is £17;

- in 1991-92 all companies had differentials greater than the target, eight of which were £50 or more;

- for 1995-96 all except three companies (Southern, Northumbrian and Severn Trent) have a differential equal to, or less than, the target.

Measured standing charges

Standing charges for some metered customers have in the past been too high, contributing to the considerable difference between the charges paid by measured and unmeasured customers, particularly households. If standing charges are too high, the ability of a customer to save money by reducing the amount of water used is limited. Unfair metered tariffs also act as a disincentive for those wishing to save money by installing a meter.

Ofwat's *1995-96 Report on tariff structure and charges* stated that measured standing charges should only recover customer-related costs, ie costs which relate to the number of customers, rather than the amount of water delivered. For measured customers these costs include meter reading and billing and the provision, maintenance and replacement of the meter. Ofwat estimates customer-related costs to be at most £32 for both water and sewerage services (in 1995-96 prices), split on a two thirds/one third basis to give £21 for water and no more than £11 for sewerage, again in 1995-96 prices.

Of the 21 water only companies:

- all companies have reduced their measured standing charges since 1991-92;

- in 1991-92, 12 companies had measured standing charges of £50 or more;

- for 1995-96, the highest measured standing charge will be £36.

Of the ten water and sewerage companies:

- since 1991-92, eight companies have reduced their measured standing charges;

- in 1991-92, four companies had standing charges of more than £100;

- for 1995-96, all companies have reduced their standing charges to less than £65, except three (Northumbrian, North West and Wessex) who include a charge for surface and highway drainage within the standing charge.

Although companies have reduced measured standing charges, these remain generally too high. The Director General will continue to press companies to reduce these further, to a level which reflects customer-related costs.

Metering

In 1989 there were only around 170,000 metered households, now the figure is almost one and a half million. Over 7 per cent of households are now metered and the figure is rising.

The Government has recently announced that water metering is, in the long term, the best basis of charging for water and sewerage services and companies should extend the availability of meters as far as is reasonable. This will take time to achieve and so legislation will be introduced to allow the existing system of calculating bills on the basis of rateable values to be used as a basis of charge after 2000.

The Director General welcomes this announcement. It is now even more important that companies have measured tariffs which are

A still from Anglian Water's video 'Metering Today' which shows the cost of using water for everyday activities. Photo: courtesy of Anglian Water

fair and which allow customers to influence the size of their bills.

Metering ensures that those customers who use more water have to meet the costs of providing extra water rather than the costs being met by all customers as at present. From the customers' viewpoint the main argument linking metering and economy must be the opportunity it offers to choose how much water they use and therefore to control their bills. Metering plays an important part in water conservation as an alternative to resource development such as reservoir construction, thereby limiting the effect on the environment such schemes can have. Metering also helps to detect leaks as everyone becomes more conscious of the amount of water used - both the customer who notices a leak on his own supply pipe and the company which has better information with which to identify areas of high leakage.

The Director General does not advocate a crash programme of universal metering, as the cost would be prohibitive. He does, however, believe that metering should be undertaken where installation is cheap, for example in new properties, where work is being undertaken on communication pipes and where properties have been substantially altered. He also believes that it would be sensible to meter large users (for example sprinkler users) and for a company to undertake more widespread metering where there are resource problems. In addition, he believes that if a meter is installed for the water service, then it should also be the basis of charge for the sewerage service.

Optional metering schemes

The Government's announcement on future charging methods has made it even more important that companies offer optional metering schemes which are customer-friendly and reasonably priced.

Customers who wish to opt for a meter have to meet the installation costs. If the installation costs and other terms and conditions are unreasonable this is unfair and could act as a disincentive - leaving customers in effect trapped in the unmeasured charging system where they may be paying for more water than they have used.

In 1991 Ofwat reviewed and compared companies' meter option schemes and found that too often company installation charges were unreasonable and accompanied by inflexible terms and conditions with limited choices over meter location or who could carry out the installation. Ofwat asked companies to improve their schemes and, in particular, to reduce the cost to customers. Guidelines on optional metering were issued to water companies in 1992. The guidelines sought to ensure that all customers have access to a reasonably priced and customer-friendly meter option.

Comparative information published on the 1994-95 schemes showed many schemes had improved. A comparison of the 1995-96 schemes (published in the Ofwat *1995-96 Report on tariff structure and charges*) reveals that companies have continued to improve their meter option schemes as a result of the Ofwat guidelines, the publication of comparative information about meter option schemes (over two successive years) and continued pressure from CSCs. Some further progress needs to be made however, especially by some companies who do not yet fully meet Ofwat's guidelines.

The main improvements since last year are:

- 14 companies have reduced their charges for installing an optional meter; in some cases by as much as 50 per cent;

- 14 companies have frozen their meter option charges, five of these for the second year running; and

- only two companies have increased their prices since 1994-95 (North East Water and North West Water).

Average charges for installing optional meters have reduced since last year (1994-95) by up to 14 per cent. The average charge for installing a meter in the highway/pavement is now 19 per cent lower than it was before Ofwat's guidelines were issued.

There is even more choice for customers over meter location; only two companies now offer customers no flexibility whatsoever over meter location compared with four last year.

The option for customers to organise the installation themselves is also more widely available; a further three companies have introduced a DIY option in 1995-96 leaving only six companies who do not have this option. A further two companies have introduced arrangements for customers to pay by instalments. This means that all companies except one, North West Water, now have these arrangements.

Twenty companies now provide a meter option costing accessible to most or all of their customers costing less than £150 (including VAT). Last year only 13 companies had prices below this 'benchmark'. Ofwat continues to believe that all companies should be able to meet and improve on this benchmark. Of particular concern is that, of the 11 companies who charge more than £150 including VAT to instal an optional meter, five charge customers in excess of £200 for the installation and one company (Southern Water) offers no capacity for the customer to shop around to get a better price because it will not allow DIY installations.

Companies who currently charge in excess of £200 (including VAT) for installing an optional meter are Northumbrian Water, York Waterworks plc, Southern Water Service Limited and Portsmouth Water plc. The Director General has told those companies with unacceptable meter option schemes that he expects improvements to be made.

Cost reflective tariffs

Ofwat will continue discussions with companies on other tariff issues such as the balance between water and sewerage services and within the sewerage service, the balance between foul drainage and surface/highway drainage, and between domestic sewerage charges and trade effluent charges.

Severn Trent Water educates customers about the cost of using water through a poster campaign in Spring 1995.
Photo: courtesy of Severn Trent Water

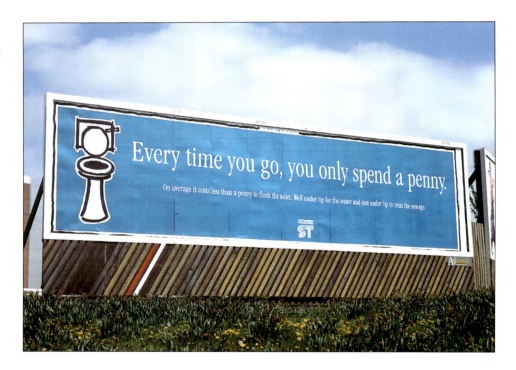

The balance between water and sewerage services

For the ten water and sewerage companies, it is important that the charges made for water and sewerage properly recover the costs of providing each service, ie no cross-subsidisation occurs. This is particularly important where companies provide only one service to a number of their customers, eg Southern Water has just over 1.6 million sewerage customers, compared with 941,000 water customers.

When the Director General set price limits last July he published indicative K factors for water and sewerage services. Due to the impact of meeting new legal obligations, these were generally higher for sewerage than water over the next ten years. This means that for most customers, sewerage bills should rise more quickly than water bills, which may fall in real terms as companies provide the service more efficiently.

Charges for sewerage services cover three elements:

- foul drainage

- surface drainage (run-off from properties)

- highway drainage (run-off from roads and pavements)

Many customers receive all three of these services. Ideally, where a customer receives only a part of the whole service, companies should charge appropriately for the service that is provided. While the Director General recognises that companies may find it difficult to split the costs of these services, he will in the summer be asking all companies about their approach to charging for sewerage services.

The Director General also wishes to ensure that there is a proper balance between domestic sewerage charges and trade effluent charges. Companies have been asked to explain how they allocate costs between these two services. One way of gauging whether charges are broadly in balance may be to compare a bill for measured domestic sewerage services with a bill for the same volume and strength of trade effluent. If charges are in balance, then these should be the same. Where they are not the same, companies will be asked to explain the reasons why.

In other industries increased competition helps to ensure that charges more accurately reflect costs. As a result of the framework set out in *Paying for water: the way ahead*, and the provisions in the Competition and Service (Utilities) Act, to facilitate competition, companies are having to examine their cost structures to check whether charges are cost reflective. If not, they risk losing such customers to competitors.

Competition in the supply of water and sewerage services takes two forms, first inset appointments and second cross boundary competition whereby a company is obliged to respond to requests for domestic water from any customer regardless of their location.

The Director General has the power to grant inset appointments for greenfield sites and for large customers (those consuming 250 megalitres of water a year or more). An inset can be granted to an existing undertaker, to a new entrant to the industry or indeed to the customer concerned (via an affiliated company). Under these provisions the competitor would have to make arrangements for a supply to be available to the site in question and would have the power to lay mains in the event of an inset appointment being agreed in principle. Given the expense

Charges for sewerage services

Trade effluent

Competition, large user tariffs and bulk supplies

involved in pipe laying, a cheaper option could be via an arrangement for a bulk supply with a local company. The Director General has the power to determine the terms and conditions of such bulk supply agreements in the event of the parties concerned failing to agree between themselves.

Ofwat has received three formal applications for inset appointments, all coupled with the request to the Director General to determine a bulk supply from the local company. As yet none of these cases has been concluded. Ofwat also receives frequent informal enquiries on this subject and expects to receive further formal applications in the near future.

Given the threat posed by inset appointments some companies have been moved to introduce a large user tariff. Within the workings of the Tariff Basket companies may rebalance charges if costs have not been properly allocated in the past. If, however, a company loses a customer to an inset appointee any loss of revenue could not be retrieved through a compensating adjustment elsewhere in the company's tariff structure.

Ofwat does not believe that unit charges should be lower for business customers merely because they use a large amount of water. There are not believed to be significant economies of scale involved in the abstraction, storage and treatment of water.

Tony Ballance and Dawn Harrison from Ofwat's Charging Policy and Research Team

There may, however, be economies of distribution which relate to the delivery of large quantities of water to a single customer or a group of customers (ie it would appear to be cheaper to supply customers who take water from large pipes before water passes through the local distribution system). In other words, there is a case for saying that for the supply of water there is a 'bulk price' or a 'wholesale price', which is the price which reflects the continuing costs of delivering large quantities of water to a single point of delivery. There is also a 'retail price' which applies to customers using the local distribution system.

The companies should be able to identify where these characteristics are material and where this is the case, Ofwat would expect to see them reflected in the tariffs. Any separate tariff should be published and made available to all customers in similar positions, not established by special agreement.

From April 1995, for water services, 18 of the 31 companies will have separate tariffs for large users within their charges schemes. One company (South West) will also have a separate sewerage tariff for large users.

There has also been interest in cross boundary competition, for example, in Croydon where the possibility was explored of households close to a company boundary seeking a water supply from a neighbouring company. To date the parties concerned have not found a route within the current legislation to make this a feasible option for them.

Cleaning Thames Water ring main.
Photo: courtesy Thames Water plc

Disconnections

If customers do not pay their water bills water companies have legal powers to disconnect their supply. To protect customers from the inappropriate use of this power a provision in the licence (Condition H) requires each company to prepare a code of practice which explains the procedure it must follow before a disconnection can be made. This procedure is common to all companies.

Following concerns about the number of county court summonses and judgements issued by companies in 1991, Ofwat undertook a review of company practice and developed guidelines which were issued in April 1992. They were designed to ensure that companies are consistent in their practice and that procedures are fair. The guidelines have offered companies, CSCs and other interested parties a clear outline of the essential elements of practice which Ofwat expects every company to follow; they supplement the minimum steps required by the licence, before a customer can be disconnected for non-payment.

Since the guidelines were issued Ofwat and the CSCs have continued to monitor companies' procedures and practice. A report on the national picture was published in spring 1993. Subsequently CSCs have kept company policies under review. A number of CSCs are auditing company records of individual disconnections. The development of these guidelines and Ofwat's continued work in this area has relied on the ability to compare and contrast company performance.

Ofwat has also undertaken two annual surveys (1991-92 and 1992-93) on the number of customers experiencing the different debt recovery stages. Ofwat used these surveys as the basis for developing enhanced reporting requirements for this area. Every six months companies must report to Ofwat both the number of disconnections for non-payment (showing the number of domestic and non-domestic customers disconnected) and the number involving unmeasured and measured customers and the duration of disconnections. Companies must also report the number of pre-summons notices, summonses and judgments issued in the year. These figures are published by Ofwat and are used to identify the overall national trend in disconnections and the rate of disconnection (a fairer measure of comparisons between companies), variations in disconnection figures and rates in CSC regions and companies and the underlying level of customers experiencing formal debt recovery action.

In 1994-95 domestic disconnections were less than half their level in 1991-92 (the year before Ofwat guidelines were issued). The 1994-95 figure for all disconnections of 12,832 is below the pre-privatisation level of 15,255 in 1988-89.

Despite the significant reduction in disconnections over the past three years and progressive improvements in the procedures of some companies, there remain significant variations between the rates of disconnections made by different companies. Towards the end of 1994-95 the Policy Studies Institute (PSI) published a report of their research into water debt and disconnection. This showed the number of households experiencing arrears with their water and sewerage bills had increased significantly since 1989. This provided support for Ofwat's early concerns about the increase in the number of customers experiencing debt recovery action. The report also commented that the fall in disconnections, in spite of the continued increase in debt, was likely to be a consequence of changes in water companies' disconnection policies as a result of the Ofwat guidelines. This study indicated support for the view, which Ofwat expressed in 1992, that high levels of water disconnection were related to the recession, the real increases in water charges and the separation of water bills from the rent paid by council tenants.

The PSI study went on to suggest that variations in the rate of disconnection between companies were due to differences in company procedures. In principle Ofwat agrees with this view to the extent that the eventual rate of disconnection is clearly influenced by the steps that a company takes and the effectiveness with which it is able to make contact with customers to reach payment agreement for repaying the debt and thus avoiding the need for disconnection.

It is not fair, however, to suggest that all companies who have high rates of disconnection are not doing enough. Nevertheless, in some of the cases, where companies have had persistently high rates of disconnection, Ofwat and the CSCs regard this as a clear indication of a need for the companies to improve their procedures. CSCs have continued to both pursue and achieve improvements in these cases throughout the past year and will continue to do so. More CSCs are undertaking audits of company records relating to disconnections. These audits have thrown light on aspects of company procedures that need to be reviewed or revised. The Director General supports those CSCs who have decided to adopt this approach and welcomes the fact that some companies, but regrettably not all of those who have been approached by their CSCs, have been supportive and open about the audit process. The Director General expects companies and CSCs to continue to work together on this important issue over the coming year.

Trials of electronic water budget units (commonly referred to as pre-payment meters) continued during the year. At the end of March 1995 11 companies were trialing these units and a further five companies were planning trials. Just over 4,000 units have been installed in customers' homes, most of these by Welsh Water, Severn Trent Water and North West Water.

Budget payment units

Ofwat and the CSCs have kept a watching brief on developments and Ofwat has collected information from companies about the number of budget payment units in use. Companies will be asked to report this information every six months with their disconnection figures.

Over the last three years all companies conducting trials have consulted CSCs and provided reports to them as the trials have progressed. The Central CSC and North West CSC have, in particular, been involved in specific monitoring and consultation arrangements throughout the course of the trials undertaken by Severn Trent Water and North West Water.

In the summer the water industry associations (WSA and WCA) developed a Code of Practice on budget payment units. The Code describes, in general terms, the basis upon which this payment method would be offered to and used by customers. Ofwat welcomed the development of the Code and CSCs have discussed its application at the local level with companies in their region who were planning to offer budget payment units. Ofwat attaches importance to companies using the WSA/WCA Code of Practice on budget payment units as a means of defining the levels of service they will provide for customers using this payment system. Ofwat expects companies to continue to discuss the detailed application of this code with the CSC for their region.

In the autumn Severn Trent Water made public the results of research by MORI into the experience and views of customers who had been trialing Severn Trent's budget payment system, Waterkey. The research found that 89 per cent of customers were satisfied with this payment system and 88 per cent would like to continue using this method of payment. These results are consistent with customer feedback and research from the trials in other areas. This has indicated that customers have been highly satisfied with this payment system and felt that it gave them particular benefits, especially in helping them to budget more effectively to pay their bills.

The year has also seen further strong evidence from the electricity industry that the availability of similar payment systems has continued to lead to very significant reductions in disconnections.

Ofwat intends to set out its views on the future use of budget payment units shortly.

CHAPTER · CHAPTER · 5

Good information is a vital component of regulation. This chapter looks at changes in Ofwat's information requirements and the introduction of output monitoring. It also details changes to the levels of service against which companies report. Ofwat's methods of communication with the companies are covered and the chapter also sets out Ofwat's work in ensuring ring-fencing of the finances of the core business. The oversight of disposals of surplus land has continued as has investigation of complaints about anti-competitive practice.

Ofwat agreed that the companies' data submissions which formed part of the defined annual reporting cycle in July each year could be delayed from July 1994 until October 1994 because of the need for Ofwat to give priority to the Periodic Review.

In October therefore Ofwat analysed information on progress on:

- capital expenditure

- operating expenditure

- levels of service

- performance measures and levels of activity

- key compliance programmes.

- regulatory accounts for 1993-94

The company returns include confidential reports and formal certificates from an independent reporter.

In December 1994 Ofwat published its three main reports based on the companies' returns (*1993-94 Report on the cost of water delivered and sewage collected, 1993-94 Report on financial performance and capital investment* and the *1993-94 Report on levels of service*). Ofwat will continue to publish these reports, together with a report on tariffs and charges based on information submitted annually with the Principal Statement in February.

Annual reporting cycle - 1993-94 Returns to the Director General

The Comparative Efficiency team from Costs and Performance Division

Independent reporting

The information submitted by companies is independently validated as a form of quality assurance. Provisions for this are laid down in the licence.

Since 1990 the companies have appointed external consultants who oversee the information submitted in the annual July Return and confirm its adequacy, accuracy and integrity. These appointments have been approved by Ofwat. Great stress has been placed on the need for expertise, independence, impartiality and professionalism.

Reporters played an important part in the Periodic Review process. It is intended that their role will continue as Ofwat's approach to monitoring performance moves more towards a system of output monitoring. Ofwat ran a number of workshops for Reporters and Auditors during the year to discuss the development of the reporting system with them. A full listing of Reporters is shown in Appendix 5.

Changes to information requirements and output monitoring

Ofwat has signalled its intention to focus increasingly on measures of output that companies achieve and to use these as a means of determining the success of a company in meeting its targets and obligations.

Ofwat has thought carefully about what information it needs to enable the Director General to comply with his statutory duties and also about the volume of information required. Too much data can lead to a descent into detail which is not productive. It is the quality of information which is important.

In May 1995 the Director General published a paper *Information for regulation* setting out his views on the information he would need to operate an output orientated regulatory regime.

Plastic pipe sections arrive from Norway at Fleetwood as part of North West Water's £500 million clean-up of the North West coast. Photo: Courtesy of North West Water.

Information needs to provide for comparisons between companies as well as for consistent time series. Some of it needs to be collected annually to measure progress with delivery of customer service. Some can be collected less frequently in preparation for a price review every five or ten years.

Discussions have been held with the quality regulators (the NRA and the DWI) about how they will provide information to Ofwat on company compliance with environmental standards.

Ofwat considers companies should demonstrate progress towards compliance with quality obligations through a system of key 'milestones' rather than simply assert that they will achieve compliance by the due date.

Ofwat has also given thought to the degree of confidentiality of information collected. Access to information on company performance is an important regulatory and public interest issue. The Director General would like to see most of the data which is collected annually made available to the public so that they can judge for themselves that their interests are being protected.

The Periodic Review emphasised the importance and value of effective systems for handling and controlling the large volume of information needed for effective regulation. Ofwat will continue to develop and build on the existing regulatory information systems.

Levels of service

Ofwat's analysis of company performance was published in *1993-94 Report on levels of service* (December 1994). This showed that during 1993-94 water companies achieved, for the third year running, an overall improvement in service to their customers, particularly in dealing with billing queries and reducing problems of low pressure. Four companies (Anglian, Thames, Mid-Kent and Yorkshire) however, were asked to explain their poor performance and submit an interim report on progress. Anglian and Thames have reported significant improvements already.

It is more important to measure what companies produce (services delivered) rather than what they spend. Ofwat has therefore considered the range of areas that affect customers directly where performance can be measured and compared. As a result, two new DG levels of service indicators will be introduced from 1995-96 onwards. These cover the frequency of meter reading and billing (DG8) and the speed at which companies answer telephone calls (DG9).

Estimated bills generate a significant number of complaints in the gas and electricity industries. With the increased level of metering in the water industry, a similar result is likely. The new DG8 indicator will record the number of customers who receive bills based on meter readings and those who receive only estimated bills during the year.

The majority of customers (as many as 80 percent in a MORI poll conducted for Ofwat in 1992) contact their water company by telephone in the first instance. The new DG9 indicator will measure how easy it is for customers to get through by telephone. It will cover the speed of answering and whether there are long periods when the lines are all busy.

In addition the scope of DG3 (water supply interruptions) will be widened to include unplanned supply interruptions of six hours or more - the current lowest band is 12 hours. DG5 (sewer flooding) will be extended to cover properties at risk of flooding more frequently than once in ten years (the current level is twice in ten years). More information will be collected on the actual occurrence of property flooding; and there will also be minor changes to other measures to improve consistency of reporting. Companies and Ofwat's CSCs were consulted about these changes.

The first opportunity to report on these new and revised measures will be in the *1996 Report on levels of service*, due to be published in the autumn of 1996.

Communication with the companies

Communication between Ofwat and the companies takes place at several levels. Major policy statements are conveyed to the companies by the Director General via the MD series of letters. The RD series of letters cover more technical and practical issues of regulation. Both series are available on subscription to the public. (A list of MD/RD letters issued during the year is given in Appendix 2).

Bill Emery (centre), Ofwat's Head of Costs and Performance with Jean Spencer, Regulatory and Accounting Controller at Yorkshire Water and Steve Procter, the company's Head of Policy and Planning. Photo: courtesy of Yorkshire Water.

Ofwat intends to continue its open and consulative approach to regulation.

Written communication is supplemented by meetings with the companies. Following the Periodic Review, the Director General resumed his practice of meeting companies to discuss issues of general and company-specific concern. The current series of meetings will be the last undertaken before the Director General's term of office ends in June 1996.

The format of these visits has been changed from previous visits. A larger Ofwat team now accompanies the

Director General. The team comprises the senior managers of Ofwat's functional teams and a member of staff (the company advisor) who takes a special interest in the activities of that particular company. The meeting also takes place at the company's premises. Visits to the water only companies last just over half a day with a whole day spent with the water and sewerage companies. It is intended that this approach, although more demanding of Ofwat's resources, will encourage the development of wider contacts between Ofwat and the companies.

Working groups

A further level of communication takes place through the Director General's working groups. The senior working groups - for accounting on regulation (WGAR) and asset management planning (WGAMP) - were valuable during preparation for the Periodic Review but have not met in the last year. Following discussion with the industry, the Director General has decided to establish a single senior group in place of the previous groups. This group will focus on important issues of regulatory policy rather than technical issues. It will not take the place of direct contact between the Director General and each individual company. It is intended that the group should meet approximately three times a year.

Ring-fencing

Companies are under a statutory duty to ensure that the appointed water and sewerage businesses are ring-fenced, that is, that they are set up in such a way that the appointed business is completely separate from the other group companies and is also independently managed and resourced from the rest of the group.

Appointees are required to provide with their Regulatory accounts each year a certificate stating that they have sufficient financial and managerial resources to carry out their functions. Companies are required to supply a further certificate to this effect, under Condition F6A of their licences, once they become aware that a material diversification is planned or has happened. Condition F has relied on a high level of self-regulation, and implies that Directors of the Appointee consider each diversification undertaken by their group to determine if it is material for Condition F6A purposes.

Diversification, in the past, has tended to be dominated by acquisitions of subsidiary companies. In practice, diversifications have encompassed joint ventures, consortia and strategic shareholdings in addition to acquisitions of subsidiaries. In response to this, the Director General has requested Appointees, when appropriate, to confirm that their Board will, in future, assess the impact of financial resources of any type of diversification they undertake and provide certificates accordingly.

Transfer pricing

Transfer prices are the prices that are paid by the appointed water and sewerage business for services supplied by associated companies.

Guidelines have been prepared (RAG 5) to assist companies to comply with amendments made to Condition F of companies' licences in March 1993 which prohibit cross-subsidy between the appointed business and non-appointed activities or any associated company. The guidelines cover the way in which transfer prices are prepared, the benefits of market testing to determine transfer prices, and the way in which costs should be allocated between the appointed and non-appointed business.

In September 1994 companies provided implementation plans and financial information describing transactions between the appointed business and associates to Ofwat.

The guidelines issued by Ofwat describe the key principles companies should follow in implementing the law. The implementation plans provided to Ofwat by individual companies showed that the quality and scope of individual company plans was very variable. To add to the information, a series of meetings was held with each of the water and sewerage companies and each of the larger water only companies if owned by a larger group. As a result of these meetings, a clearer view has been formed of the extent of current company compliance with RAG 5 and implementation proposals for the future.

There are a number of areas where further reporting will be required in future years from the companies. They are currently required to report on transactions with associated companies and on individual transactions which exceed company set materiality levels, or where reductions to these materiality levels have been made. Companies will, in future, be required to report more fully on all contracts with associates above £1 million.

Companies have reported on transactions with associates taking place within the financial year. In future companies will be asked to comment on the value and duration of contracts with associates that extend beyond a single financial year.

In addition to the annual reporting requirements agreed with companies, a programme of checks on companies' activities in this area will be instituted. These checks will be carried out by a team of consultants under the guidance of Ofwat staff. The first of these will occur in the autumn of 1995. These checks will form part of an annual rolling cycle. It is anticipated that most of the companies will be visited within two years. Checks will be made on specific areas of company activity. This may include such areas as procurement policy and practice, determination of market price with associates, strategic contracts, cost allocation and the level of activity based costing. CSCs will also be asked whether they have any information which should be fed into the checks. The selection of companies will be random and it is not intended that checks will be deliberately geared towards companies whose compliance with RAG 5 is less well developed than others, although all companies will be visited in time. Individual companies will be required to amend their systems to comply with the guidelines if the checks show they are not doing so already. The consultants undertaking these checks will be required to prepare a report on their findings to Ofwat. In turn, the results of these checks will be presented to the industry and the public as guidance for ensuring their systems are compliant. If shortcomings to the guidelines or areas that require strengthening became evident, amendments to the guidelines will be made to reflect these. The results of these checks will be reported in next year's Annual Report.

Anti-competitive practices

Ofwat receives and investigates complaints of anti-competitive practice. The Director General has powers concurrent with the Director General of Fair Trading to investigate complaints of anti-competitive practice and a small number of complaints are passed to Ofwat by the Office of Fair Trading.

Complaints tend to take the form of telephone or written complaints. Because of the seriousness of the issue, Ofwat will only investigate an allegation of anti-competitive practice with a water or water and sewerage company where the allegation is made in the form of a written complaint. In practice only a small number of written complaints are made. The majority of those complaining allege that associate companies of appointed water and sewerage companies have an advantage compared to market competitors as they have guaranteed work with the appointed business which gives them an advantage over their competitors in the open market. Companies often appear to be unwilling to make a formal complaint to Ofwat as they consider that setting a complaint in motion will adversely affect their chances of gaining any work that is tendered in the market by the company against whom an allegation is made. A number of complaints have been investigated in the last financial year. None of the companies investigated were found to have acted anti-competitively.

When alleging either anti-competitive practice or that an associate is being cross-subsidised, complainants are asked to provide as much information in support of their complaint as they can, as well as information about the market in which they operate. Companies against whom the complaint is made are then asked to respond to the allegation and provide additional information to enable Ofwat to determine if the complainants concerns are justified. Several exchanges of letters involving both the complainant and the relevant company are usually involved.

In pursuing a complaint a company may be asked to present the case at a meeting with Ofwat staff. If the Director General considers that a complaint is well-founded, he can ask a company to undertake to desist from the offending practice. If the Director considers that an anti-competitive practice is occurring, but that it is beyond his jurisdiction, he can pass the complaint on to the Office of Fair Trading.

Mergers

On 31 December 1994 the special shares in each of the water and sewerage companies held by the Secretary of State for the Environment, were redeemed at par (£1). These shares were frequently referred to as the 'golden share'. Prior to this, any one shareholder in the water and sewerage companies was limited to a 15 per cent stake.

The redemption of the golden share allows mergers and takeovers to occur amongst the water and sewerage companies. This has always been the case for the water only companies. The only exception to this, at present, is Welsh Water plc for whom a national interest case was maintained at privatisation and hence a special resolution by the shareholders would be required to relinquish the golden share.

The possibility for mergers and competition for corporate control gives rise to two avenues for potential mergers, each with different implications. The first of these is a merger between two or more water or water and sewerage companies. Any merger of this type between companies each with assets of more than £30 million is automatically referred to the MMC. The first bid for a water and sewerage company has come from Lyonnaise des Eaux. Lyonnaise already owns two water only companies (North East Water and Essex and Suffolk) and the bid has been referred to the MMC for them to consider the comparative competition aspects. Market competition issues will be considered by the EC as the bid falls within European competition rules.

The second type of merger that could occur is between a water or a water and sewerage company and a non-water enterprise. In this circumstance a reference to the MMC would only take place if the Secretary of State considered it could be against the public interest on other competition grounds.

In the case of a bid from a non-water enterprise, the Director General would seek to ensure that the company wishing to take over the water company is fit and proper to manage a water or water and sewerage company and is able properly to carry out its functions and to finance them.

Unless a specific consent is obtained from the Secretary of State, all land disposals by water companies must comply with Condition K of the companies' licences. The purpose of Condition K is two-fold: to ensure that the land to be disposed is surplus and that the 'best price' is obtained for the land, usually certified by independent valuers. Companies are required to notify and seek Ofwat's consent if the disposal is valued above £500,000. In these cases they must supply certificates with independent valuations. Ofwat scrutinises the documents to ensure that the valuers' assessments are realistic, particularly with regard to the planning potential of the land.

The year has seen continuing activity on transfers of land between associated companies. Fewer disposals have been made than in previous years but of higher value sites. In 1993-94, 108 disposals were valued at £20 million; in 1994-95 54 disposals were valued at £28 million. Few sites have reached the values that were allowed for in setting price limits in 1989.

Tables 15 and 16 show more detailed figures for the financial year April 1994 to March 1995.

Property development and land disposal

TABLE 15 VALUE OF DISPOSALS BY CSC REGION	TABLE 16 NUMBER OF CASES BY CSC REGION

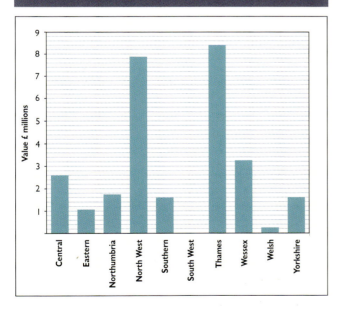

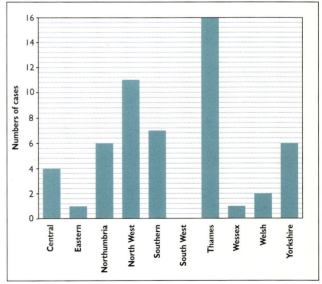

Note:

The tables include leases, where they are categorised as disposals of land, as well as outright sales. In many cases, substantial further payments will accrue to the core companies in later years as clawback conditions become operative. Conversely, some disposals notified to Ofwat may be subsequently withdrawn before completion. The tables do not include all disposals made by water companies, as arm's length disposals under £500,000 need not be notified under Condition K but are reported annually in the July Return

Adjustments were made for a number of companies in the Periodic Review to allow for this loss of revenue. No assumptions were made concerning proceeds from land sales in the new K factors so all proceeds in future years will be eligible for sharing between customers and shareholders of companies.

The trend towards bulk transfers of surplus sites to associated property development companies continues. A further two water and sewerage companies made such transfers during the period under review. Clawback provisions have been included in most of these transactions, as usual. In addition, proceeds from earlier clawback provisions are now starting to show in the accounts of core companies, as sites are developed and sold on.

Typical examples of cases dealt with in this period:

- Proposals to redevelop 16 acres of a former sewage works in the Midlands as a retail park. To increase the ability of the site to attract passing trade, a number of frontage dwellings will have to be acquired for demolition and landscaping. The remainder of the site has already been developed for housing and a football stadium, together with associated car parking and a social club.

- Representations at a local plan inquiry, a High Court action and two planning appeals finally achieved planning consent for residential development on a former sewage works near Fareham in Hampshire. Consent enabled the exercise of an option granted in favour of an associated property company three years previously.

The Periodic Review was a large and complex project, which brought with it considerable intellectual and managerial challenges. In the light of this, and as a matter of good project management practice, Ofwat undertook a review of its overall approach to the Periodic Review and its management of the process.

The 1994 Periodic Review, which culminated in the Director General's announcement of new price limits for the next decade for the 31 companies in England and Wales, was a major undertaking for Ofwat. It involved a significant proportion of its staff over a period of three years. Two companies (South West and Portsmouth) asked for their price limits to be referred to the MMC for re-determination.

The National Audit Office described the initial K-setting exercise at the time of privatisation as 'unprecedented in its magnitude and complexity'. Resetting price limits for 31 companies was no less daunting.

The primary purpose of this review was to identify and document the lessons learnt. The outcomes are already informing Ofwat's thinking on how it works with the companies and others, as well as how the Office itself operates, particularly in terms of good project management practice.

The review involved all Ofwat's key stakeholders: its staff, the Ofwat National Customer Council, the companies and their Reporters, as well as representatives of the City, the media and customer and business organisations. A survey of customer awareness was also carried out via the regular OPCS omnibus survey.

Ofwat's principal achievement lay in establishing and managing a process which delivered 31 separate determinations in a confidential environment on the planned date of 28 July 1994. The average of those determinations lay within the narrow band of Ks between 0 to 2 which the Director General considered affordable, in the light of customer consultations.

Ofwat's achievements

Ofwat was also instrumental in raising the cost of quality debate at government level, arguing for the costs of implementation to be considered explicitly when Ministers consider new and proposed environmental legislation.

The views of customers were fed into the Periodic Review process to a greater extent than ever before, both via the Market Plan exercise which Ofwat encouraged the companies to carry out and through the close involvement of the ten CSC chairmen. This level of involvement is reflected in the benefits Ofwat has secured for customers:

- bills will rise at a significantly slower rate than would otherwise have been the case; in some cases, bills will fall in real terms;

- companies will be investing very large sums of money to meet their legal quality obligations, which will generate both environmental benefits and improvements in water quality;

- customers will receive more for their money as a result of efficiency improvements by the companies.

The review of the Periodic Review has indicated that the process Ofwat undertook generally won respect for its professionalism. There are, of course, lessons to be learnt for the future.

Learning points

A wide range of issues was raised by those who participated in the review, both at a strategic and detailed level. Despite this, it has been possible to draw out a small number of major issues and common themes from their comments.

The companies considered there was an incongruity between the volume of data they were asked to submit to Ofwat, and the information provided by Ofwat to support its decisions on price limits.

Ofwat is considering the possible implications of this as part of its planning for future data submissions, as well as looking at issues such as the clarity and consistency of the guidance provided to companies and the efficiency of data capture systems.

The companies felt that, although the general principles of the methodology were clearly set out, there was a lack of transparency as to how those principles would be (or were) applied.

Ofwat explained its approach with as much clarity and openness as reasonable. The process of setting prices, however, cannot be mechanistic; the Director General had to have scope to reach his own informed judgements. Ofwat will be considering how it may be able to communicate the nature, and key aspects, of its approach at an earlier stage in future.

Ofwat published a series of consultation papers on key elements in its approach between 1991 and 1994. These papers also sought to discuss major elements of its approach directly with the industry. Some recipients of the papers felt that Ofwat used its consultation process more to inform the industry and others rather than prompt a dialogue with the water companies.

One of the points raised by the consumer and business organisations was that they were not always entirely clear of the Periodic Review process and their role in it. Some felt unable to comment on what they perceived to be a rather technical debate. Organisations would like to have seen published the results of Ofwat's consultation exercises.

Ofwat will consider how to ensure the industry and other interested parties understand the issues for consultation and how they fit into the overall process.

Some of the public documents produced by the companies following the Periodic Review

The companies were disappointed with the process and outcome of the Market Plan exercise, both in terms of its timing (ie before the extent and cost of quality obligations had been established), and in the way they considered it created expectations that the influence of the Plans on the Director General's determinations would be more explicit leading to higher price limits. Some of the consumer organisations felt that Ofwat should have been more prescriptive about how companies consulted their customers or even should have carried out the research itself to ensure a consistent approach.

A survey in January 1995 showed a reasonably high level of awareness amongst customers about company Market Plans and Ofwat's role in setting price limits. To that extent the exercise was successful in involving customers.

The Market Plan exercise deliberately encouraged companies to decide for themselves how to assess the views of their customers and to carry out their own research; Ofwat did not therefore control or direct the process. Nevertheless, there are lessons for Ofwat in limiting expectations around the publication of any future Market Plans.

These issues will be matters for consideration by the next Director General in planning the approach to, and handling of, the next Periodic Review.

Cost effectiveness of Ofwat's approach

The total cost to Ofwat of carrying out the Periodic Review has been estimated at approximately £6 million, incurred over a three-year period, covering staff and consultancy costs and expenditure on, for example, accommodation, IT and training.

As part of the review of the Periodic Review, Ofwat sought to assess the cost effectiveness of its approach using a range of available comparators.

First, Ofwat's expenditure of £6 million compares favourably with the costs incurred by the Department of the Environment and the Welsh Office at initial K-setting. Their costs were estimated to be about £12 million (1994-95 prices).

Ian Byatt with Dilys Plant, Head of Information at the Periodic Review press conference.

Secondly, the forecast costs of Ofwat's Periodic Review implied by the licence fee cap, which was set at 0.3 per cent of company turnover by the Department of the Environment, would have allowed Ofwat to collect some £15 million from companies to cover its Periodic Review costs.

Finally, one can look at the savings to customers implied by the new K factors. The average price limit arising from the 1994 Periodic Review for the five years 1995-2000 was RPI plus 1.4. This represents savings of:

- 2.3 points over the average K initially set for this period in 1989-94

- 4.8 points over the average K set out in the companies' Market Plans

Each point equates to approximately £50 million each year in terms of bills which customers pay. The cash benefit to customers arising from the success of the Periodic Review, therefore, amounts to some £115 million to £240 million each year for the next five years. In addition they will be assured of better quality, especially of waste water discharges to rivers and seas.

In the light of this analysis, it is reasonable to conclude that Ofwat undertook a process which represented value for money, both to tax payers and customers.

Communications became more important than ever. The announcement of the new price limits was the culmination of an open and transparent three year process. Ofwat's external relations strategy was designed to ensure that the key players were kept fully informed - that is, the companies, who would be responsible for delivering the service, the City, from whom the companies would attract investment, the customers who would pay the bills, the media, as well as policy makers and standard setters.

Handling the Periodic Review

Throughout the process of the Review, the Director General talked to many key journalists and the City. These meetings were aimed at increasing understanding of the Periodic Review process, to reduce speculation and to increase the opportunity for an informed and balanced debate. During the year the Director General also met many Members of Parliament to hear what they had to say about water prices and quality of service.

The announcement of the new price limits for the water industry was made via a Stock Exchange announcement and a press notice issued at 7.30 am on 28 July. Accompanying the announcement was the more detailed explanatory document, *Future Charges for Water and Sewerage Services.* The Director General then briefed the City and the national press. Regional press conferences, taken by the CSC chairmen, covered the local angle, adding strong regional messages to the national announcement. The national conference attracted over 40 journalists.

In the media

Thirty national press notices were issued (see Appendix 3) with a further 130 press notices issued by the CSCs during the year. Ofwat's active approach to the media was largely geared to the Review which received widespread coverage. But media interest did not focus only on the Review. There were other significant news stories: Ofwat announced a better deal for metered customers; pointed to metering as the way to sustainable development; announced that household disconnections had reduced by a third since 1993, and that levels of service provided by companies were improving. There were other strong messages: for the water industry, as the Director General sounded a note of caution on large dividend payouts; for the public, confirmation that investment in the industry remained high, with the companies carrying out the improvements expected when price limits were initially set in 1989; and for the government, as Ofwat pressed for a requirement on the new Environment Agency to consider costs as well as benefits, and called for legislation to promote the efficient use of water and sewerage services by the water companies.

In addition, the Director General and senior Ofwat officials gave over 100 interviews to radio and television stations. Most were to news and business programmes about the Review but others covered issues such as disconnections and customer representation, and general interest programmes such as Woman's Hour and the Jimmy Young Show. The CSC chairmen and regional managers between them gave many interviews to local media.

Ofwat's press office handled over 3,500 enquiries from the media - an increase of over 50 per cent on 1993. In addition the CSCs dealt with over 1,400 media enquiries and interviews. There was also demand for articles, from titles including Parliamentary Brief and World Statesman.

Contacts with Parliament

A new post of Parliamentary and Briefing Officer was created within Information Division as a means of improving communications between Ofwat and Members of Parliament and to foster greater understanding of the Director General's role through the preparation of briefing material.

Shows

For the third year running, Ofwat's CSCs joined forces with the electricity and telecom watchdogs to promote their customer protection messages by staging a travelling roadshow. The show visited Barnstable, Chatham, Kendal, Leeds, Wandsworth, Sunderland, Norwich, Boscombe, Hereford and Derby. Over 1,500 enquiries were dealt with during the roadshows.

Customers had another chance to meet the watchdog when Ofwat took a stand at the Cheshire, Devon, Northumberland and Royal Bath and West of England shows. Staff from Headquarters joined CSC staff to talk to around 500 visitors.

These shows increase awareness and understanding of Ofwat's role and give customers the opportunity to raise their problems and express their views, face to face.

A record number of overseas visitors were received during 1994

Overseas visitors

Ofwat received a record 50 visitors from around the world - including Europe, South and North America, Asia and Australasia, South

Africa and the West Indies - all with a special interest in regulation of the water industry. These senior officials included politicians and government officials, representatives from the water industry, other public utilities, regulators and academia.

Conferences and talks

The Director General and his staff receive invitations throughout the year to attend national conferences and seminars and to give talks and lectures to a variety of audiences at home and abroad. Some 55 engagements were accepted. Regional managers and CSC chairmen also carried out an extensive programme of speaking events to local and regional groups.

Alan Booker, Deputy Director General, addresses the Open Forum of the Food and Drink Federation.
Photo: courtesy of the Food and Drink Federation.

The role of regulation and setting price limits were the main issues for speakers. The Director General gave clear signals to the industry and to its customers that the key challenge to the companies over the next five years will be reducing the cost of existing services. The Deputy Director General, meanwhile, addressed issues including regulating the utilities in a changing marketplace and strategies for success and developments in water services.

The Review heightened interest this year. It was impossible to accept every request, but Ofwat makes every effort to provide a speaker where participation will be of value.

Talking to the City

Contacts with institutional investors increased in the approach to the Review. Two-way communication is important - and Ofwat was keen to listen to what the City had to say. City views were also sought by Ofwat during its review of the process of the Periodic Review.

1994 Publications

The key document this year was the outcome of the Periodic Review, *Future charges for water and sewerage services*. A summary leaflet was also published.

Ofwat published a new document setting out its complaints procedure, and an explanatory leaflet for customers, *Water and sewerage: how we can help if you have a complaint*, which was awarded the Plain English Campaign's Crystal Mark for clarity.

On charging for water, there were two new Ofwat reports: *A better deal for metered customers* and *Opting for a meter: a report on water company metering schemes.*

An occasional paper on *Future levels of demand and supply for water* was written at the request of the Select Committee on the Environment. Three research papers were produced on modelling sewerage and sewage treatment costs and comparing sewerage service operating expenditure.

Ofwat has updated all its leaflets and information notes following the Review. The range of notes was expanded to include subjects such as: the role of the regulator, understanding the licence, paying by meter, the structure of the industry and MMC referrals. Information notes are available free of charge. They are listed in Appendix 4.

Library services and public enquiries

The library acts as a public enquiry unit and also as the publication sales and distribution point. Approximately 8,500 enquiries were answered and about 32,000 publications were issued. Eighteen per cent of the written enquiries received were answered the same day and 44 per cent within one working day; 99 per cent of enquiries received were answered within six working days. Annual

Satvinder Sandhu from Ofwat's library, which answered 8,500 enquiries and issued 32,000 publications during the year.

subscriptions to the 'Dear Managing Director' and 'Dear Regulatory Director' letters stand at 130. About 140 requests for single copies of these letters were also received.

The public correspondence unit answers letters that are of a general nature, or concern Ofwat policy. This year 451 letters were answered, compared to 288 in 1992 - an increase of 57 per cent; 87 per cent of letters are cleared within five working days. The number of letters answered from Members of Parliament, Peers and MEPs also increased.

Ofwat received only one request under the Code of Practice on Open Government.

The Director General's Register is maintained by and housed in the Library and is freely available for consultation by the public, with a small charge made for copies of extracts.

Determinations made by the Director General under Section 45 of the Water Industry Act 1991, concerning disputes about connection charges, are now available for inspection in the Library.

The number of outside visitors using the Library for research increased by 5 per cent to 140.

OFWAT'S RESOURCES

TABLE 17 OFWAT'S BUDGET 1994-95

Ofwat's budget for 1994-95 was £9.5 million. This consisted of:

	£ millions
Running costs	**£9.1**
Staff costs	£4.8
Consultancy costs	£1.7
Accommodation costs	£0.9
Other running costs	£1.6
Capital	**£0.4**

Running cost expenditure was split between Divisions as follows:

Consumer Affairs	£0.5
CSC Appointments and Performance	£0.3
Costs and Performance	£1.1
DG & DDG	£0.7
Economic Regulation	£2.1
Information	£0.8
Legal	£0.2
Administration	£0.6
General costs	£1.0
CSC costs	£1.8

Footnote: Figures may not add due to rounding

Costs

Finance

Ofwat obtained agreement from the Chief Secretary to the Treasury for total expenditure of £9.5 million during the 1994-95 financial year, as the workload for the Periodic Review peaked in the summer. An out-turn of £9.2 million is anticipated, representing a saving of £294,000, or 3.1 per cent. Ofwat's anticipated expenditure for 1995-96 is expected to be £8.7 million representing a reduction of £531,000, or 6 per cent. Ofwat's costs are entirely covered by licence fees levied on individual water companies, apportioned on the basis of turnover of the appointed business.

Costs of the Periodic Review

Ofwat completed the Periodic Review for a total of some £6 million over the period 1992-3 to 1994-5. This was split between:

Staff costs	£3.1 million
Consultancies	£2.1 million
Other	£0.7 million.

This is equivalent to a cost of roughly 12p per household. The total is far less than was spent by DoE in the original K-setting exercise. It also compares very well with the anticipated costs of the MMC for the two references which they have considered.

Staff numbers were boosted for the duration of the Review, particularly over the nine months to July 1994. Human Resources Branch were kept busy with 20 separate recruitment exercises. A significant number of professional staff on the regulatory side of the office have since moved on to jobs outside Ofwat. This is good for regulation in general as it helps spread expertise about price setting. This, however, has to be matched by further recruitment by Ofwat to maintain an effective team.

Consultancy costs were kept under control by developing expertise in-house. Specialist advice was retained for certain areas where it was not cost effective to recruit staff with these areas of knowledge. The distinction between full time staff and consultants becomes increasingly blurred as the office develops a richer mix of contracts and contacts. Ofwat has developed a network in the regulatory world which act as sources of advice and a sounding board against which to test ideas. This helps ensure that the office learns from developments across a wider spectrum both inside and beyond the water industry.

Delegation

Ofwat welcomes the chance to take responsibility for its own pay and grading arrangements from April 1996. This is in line with a civil service wide policy. This will allow Ofwat to match market rates in the pay levels of staff. It will also give much greater flexibility to create teams that reflect the needs of the job.

Ofwat will also become responsible for the management of its own accomodation from that date. Property Holdings (part of DoE) will no longer act as an intermediary. This should give the office much greater control over the property it occupies.

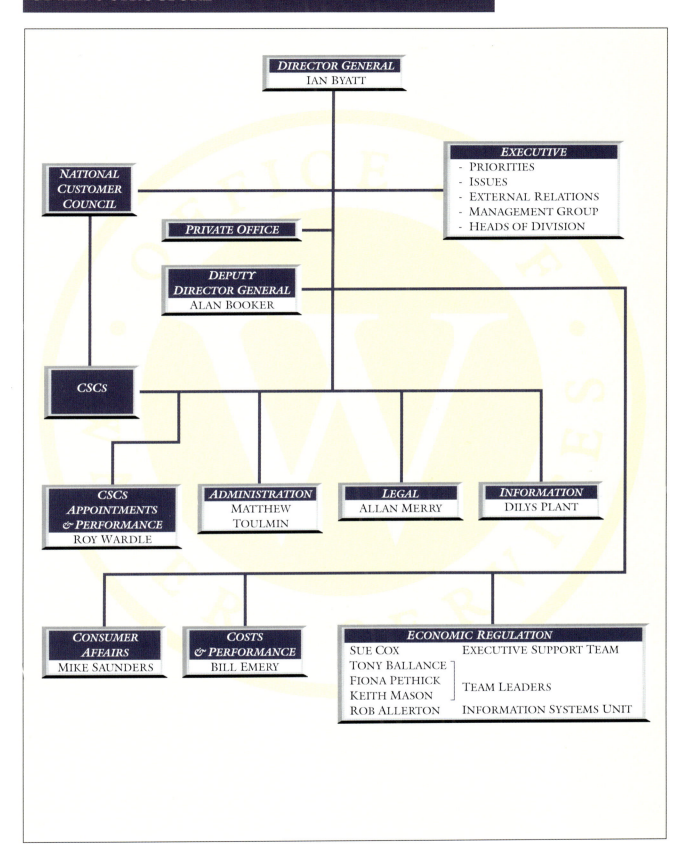

DIRECTOR GENERAL
IAN BYATT

EXECUTIVE
- PRIORITIES
- ISSUES
- EXTERNAL RELATIONS
- MANAGEMENT GROUP
- HEADS OF DIVISION

NATIONAL CUSTOMER COUNCIL

PRIVATE OFFICE

DEPUTY DIRECTOR GENERAL
ALAN BOOKER

CSCS

CSCS APPOINTMENTS & PERFORMANCE
ROY WARDLE

ADMINISTRATION
MATTHEW TOULMIN

LEGAL
ALLAN MERRY

INFORMATION
DILYS PLANT

CONSUMER AFFAIRS
MIKE SAUNDERS

COSTS & PERFORMANCE
BILL EMERY

ECONOMIC REGULATION
SUE COX — EXECUTIVE SUPPORT TEAM
TONY BALLANCE
FIONA PETHICK
KEITH MASON — TEAM LEADERS
ROB ALLERTON — INFORMATION SYSTEMS UNIT

OFWAT CUSTOMER SERVICE COMMITTEES

AT 31 MARCH 1994

Central CSC

First Floor
77 Paradise Circus
Birmingham
B1 2DZ

Responsible for customers of:
Severn Trent Water Ltd
South Staffordshire Water plc

Telephone:	0121 212 5202
Lo-call:	0345 023953
Fax:	0121 212 5204

Office hours: 8.45 - 16.45 Mon - Fri

Chairman   Mr Clive Wilkinson
Members   Mrs Diane Atton
                    Mr Gerald Godby
                    Mr Martin Hudson
                    Mr Clive Hulls
                    Mrs Mary Milton
                    Mrs Sheila Ray
                    Mr Tom Rees-Jones
                    Dr Neil Richardson
                    Mrs Sheila Rowley
                    Mrs Brenda Sharp
                    Mrs Barbara Venes

*Regional Manager
and Secretary*   Mr Will Dawson

Eastern CSC

Ground Floor
Carlyle House
Carlyle Road
Cambridge
CB4 3DN

Responsible for customers of:
Anglian Water Services Ltd
Cambridge Water Company
Essex & Suffolk Water plc
Tendring Hundred Water Services Ltd

Telephone:	01223 323889
Lo-call:	0345 9599369
Fax:	01223 323930

Office hours: 9.00 - 17.00 Mon - Fri

Chairman   Dr Roger Corbett
Members   Mr David Edgar
                    Mr David Howarth
                    Mr Bryan Johnston
                    Mr Kenneth Phillips
                    Mrs Barbara Ruffell
                    Mrs Dierdre Sanders
                    Mrs Zena Scoley
                    Mr Charles Simeons
                    Mr John Tapp
                    Mr Roy Thompson
                    Mrs Gillian Townson
                    Mrs Kathleen Weekes

*Regional Manager
and Secretary*   Mrs Jessica Jackson

Northumbria CSC

Second Floor
35 Nelson Street
Newcastle
NE1 5AN

Responsible for customers of:
Northumbrian Water Ltd
North East Water plc
Hartlepool Water plc

Telephone:	0191 221 0646
Lo-call:	0345 089367
Fax:	0191 221 0650

Office hours: 8.30 - 17.00 Mon - Thurs
8.30 - 16.30 Fri

Chairman
Members

Mr Jim Gardner CVO CBE DL
Mrs Maggie Bosanquet
Mr Ian Brown
Mr Ron Dunn
Mr David Graham
Mr Alfred Groome
Mr David Holliday
Mr Patrick Hornor
Mr Dennis Hudson
Mr Alex Lee
Mrs Ann Morris
Mr James Simpson
Mrs Mary Storer
Mr Douglas Thompson
Mr Harry Thornton
Mrs Josephine Turnbull

Regional Manager
and Secretary   Mrs Elaine Finlay

North West CSC

First Floor
Boulton House
17-21 Chorlton Street
Manchester
M1 3HY

Responsible for customers of:
North West Water Ltd

Telephone:	0161 236 6112
Lo-call:	0345 056316
Fax:	0161 228 6117

Office hours: 9.00 - 17.00 Mon - Fri

Chairman
Members

Mr Anthony Goldstone MBE DL FCA
Mrs Beryl Allan
Mr Arnold Barcroft
Mr Peter Fell
Mr Bob Gale
Mrs Lorena Hunt
Mr Richard Long
Mrs Deborah Morton
Mr Chris Muir OBE
Mr Colin Reynolds
Mrs Iris Shanahan
Miss Maureen Vince

Regional Manager
and Secretary   Ms Margaret Smith

South West CSC

First Floor
Broadwalk House
Southernhay West
Exeter
EX1 1TS

Responsible for customers of:
South West Water Services Ltd

Telephone:	01392 428028
Lo-call:	0345 959059
Fax:	01392 428010

Office hours:	8.45 - 16.45 Mon - Fri

Chairwoman	Mrs Jessica Thomas
Members	Mr Norman Bancroft
	Mr Aubrey Bourne
	Mr Roger Bowen
	Dr Stuart Coverley
	Mr Mike Cox
	Mr Adam Gifford
	Mr Geoffrey Hibbert
	Mrs Anne Mayes
	Mrs Janet Pearce
	Ms Ruth Stringer
	Mrs Elizabeth-Anne Waldron-Yeo
Regional Manager and Secretary	Mr Mark Hann

Southern CSC

Third Floor
15-17 Ridgmount Street
London
WC1E 7AH

Responsible for customers of:
Southern Water Services Ltd
Portsmouth Water plc
Mid Kent Water plc
Folkestone & Dover Water Services Ltd
South East Water Ltd

Telephone:	0171 636 3656
Lo-call:	0345 581658
Fax:	0171 637 4813

Office hours:	9.00 - 17.30 Mon - Thurs
	9.00 - 17.15 Fri

Chairman	Professor Judith Rees
Members	Mr Nick Bagnall
	Mr Mike Dobson
	Mr John Harris
	Mr Clive Howard-Luck
	Miss Heather Humby
	Dr John Lawrence
	Mr Mike Perfect
	Lady Peston
	Ms Claire Pracey
	Dr John Reader
	Mr Harry Speight
	Mrs Christine Swan
Regional Manager & Secretary	Ms Karen Gibbs

Thames CSC

Second Floor
15-17 Ridgmount Street
London
WC1E 7AH

Telephone:	0171 636 3656
Lo-call:	0345 581658
Fax:	0171 636 3665

Office hours: 9.00 - 17.30 Mon - Thurs
                9.00 - 17.15 Fri

Chairman   Mrs Elizabeth Monck
Members   Mr Clive Collier
              Mr John Hills
              Ms Suzanne Hinton
              Mr David Horton
              Mrs Sheila Kempner
              Ms Lynette Lithgow
              Mr John Moore MBE
              Mrs Diana Ratzer
              Mr Robert Russell CBE
              Mrs June Smith
              Mr Subhash Thakrar
              Mrs Glenys Thornton
              Mr Ronald Yearsley
Regional Manager
and Secretary   Mr Andrew Milne

Responsible for customers of:
Thames Water Utilities Ltd
Three Valleys Water plc
East Surrey Water plc
Mid Southern Water plc
North Surrey Water plc
Sutton District Water plc

CSC for Wales

Room 140
Caradog House
1-6 St Andrews Place
Cardiff
CF1 3BE

Telephone:	01222 239852
Lo-call:	0345 078267
Fax:	01222 239847

Office hours: 8.30 - 16.30 Mon - Fri

Chairman   The Venerable Raymond Roberts CB
Members   Mrs Nerys Hâf Biddulph
              Mrs Penny Brickle
              Mr Derek Bryer
              Dr Michael Davies
              Mrs Patricia Forrest
              Miss Maureen Holling
              Mrs Heather March
              Mr Patrick Moriarty
              Mr Stephen Powell
              Mr Maldwyn Rees
              Mrs Sheila Tristram
              Mr John Warman
Regional Manager
and Secretary   Mr Clive Sterl

Responsible for customers of:
DŵrCymru Cyfyngedig
Chester Waterworks Company
Wrexham Water plc

Wessex CSC

2 The Hide Market
West Street
St Philips
Bristol
BS2 0BH

Telephone:	0117 9557001
Lo-call:	0345 078268
Fax:	0117 9557037

Office hours:	8.45 - 16.45 Mon - Fri

Chairman	Mr Anthony Clothier
Members	David Baines MBE
	Mr Charles Barter
	Mr Piers Feilden
	Mr Alan Godson
	Mr Jeffrey Hordle
	Mr Leslie Keyte
	Mrs Brenda Lalonde
	Mr Ian Macdonald
	Mr Brian May
	Mrs Diana Tory
	Mr Graham Turner
	Mrs Jean Watkins
Regional Manager and Secretary	Mrs Teresa Evans

Responsible for customers of:
Wessex Water Services Ltd
Bournemouth & West Hampshire
    Water plc
Bristol Water plc
Cholderton & District Water
    Company Ltd

Yorkshire CSC

Ground Floor
Symons House
Belgrave Street
Leeds
LS2 8DD

Telephone:	0113 2340874
Lo-call:	0345 089368
Fax:	0113 2341316

Office hours:	8.30 - 17.00 Mon-Fri

Chairman	Mr Eric Wilson
Members	Mr Mohammed Ashraf Bismil BEM
	Mr Ian Blakey
	Mrs Jenny Clarke
	Mr Roy Collinge
	Mr John Dawson
	Ms Kath Fysh
	Mrs Penny Hemming
	Dr Thomas Morris
	Mrs Rosalind Perry
	Mr Gordon Polley MBE
Regional Manager and Secretary	Mr Andrew Mitchelson

Responsible for customers of:
Yorkshire Water Services Ltd
York Waterworks plc

LETTERS TO THE COMPANIES

1 APRIL 1994 – TO DATE

Number	Description	Dated

DEAR MANAGING DIRECTOR LETTERS

Issued during 1994

Number	Description	Dated
MD 101	Arrangements for Periodic Review	15.03.94

Issued during 1995

Number	Description	Dated
MD 102	Metering of new properties	07.02.95
MD 103	Diversification and the protection of the core business - condition FBA	13.02.95
MD 104	Incentives, benefit sharing and the investment needs of the industry	13.04.95

DEAR REGULATORY DIRECTOR LETTERS

Issued during 1994

Number	Description	Dated
RD1/94	July Return reporting requirements manual 1994 return	09.02.94
RD2/94	Strategic Business Plan - clarification of issues	11.02.94
RD3/94	Sewerage service base operating expenditure: research papers 3 and 4 and overview paper	18.02.94
RD4/94	RAG 5: Transfer pricing in the water industry	10.03.94
RD5/94	Reporters' and auditors' joint workshops quality enhancement programmes	11.03.94
RD6/94	Interest rates for requisitions and infrastructure charges - six monthly review	21.03.94
RD7/94	Optional meter schemes	23.03.94
RD8/94	Reporting of water disconnections 1993-94	12.04.94
RD9/94	Regulatory accounts for 1993-94	09.05.94
RD9A/94	Amendment to RD9	23.05.94
RD10/94	Interest rates for requisitions and infrastructure charges - interim review	23.05.94
RD11/94	Regulatory accounts for 1993-94	02.08.94
RD12/94	Personnel change - economic regulation	05.08.94

RD13/94	Reporting of water disconnections 1994-95	28.09.94
RD14/94	Review of information for customers	10.10.94
RD15/94	Interest rates for requisitions and infrastructure charges - interim review	20.10.94
RD16/94	1995-96 Principal statement	16.12.94

Issued during 1995

RD1/95	Proposed levels of service output measures	06.01.95
RD2/95	Infrastructure charges	09.01.95
RD3/95	July Return reporting requirements	27.01.95
RD4/95	Optional meter schemes - 1995-96	10.03.95
RD5/95	Reporting of water disconnections 1994-95	07.04.95
RD6/95	1993-94 report on the cost of water delivered and sewage collected	11.04.95
RD7/95	July Return 1996 - proposed levels of service output measures July Return 1995 - guidance for completion	13.04.95
RD8/95	Interest rates for requisitions and infrastructure charges interim review	25.04.95
RD9/95	Regulatory accounts for 1994-95	03.05.95

APPENDIX 3 APPENDIX

1994

1/94	More customers to benefit from proposed licence amendments	7.1.94
2/94	Proposals published for Essex Water to replace Suffolk Water	11.2.94
3/94	Chairmen for Ofwat's regional committees announced	22.2.94
4/94	Water companies have opportunity to reduce their costs says regulator	14.3.94
5/94	Next year's average water and sewerage bill in England and Wales - £199	16.3.94
6/94	Ofwat wins better deal for metered customers	24.3.94
7/94	Ofwat interferes less in changing water companies' price limits	29.3.94
8/94	Three Valleys Water merger completed this week	30.3.94
9/94	Essex Water to replace Suffolk Water	30.3.94
10/94	South East Water replaces West-Kent, Mid-Sussex and Eastbourne Water	30.3.94
11/94	New Chairman of Ofwat Eastern appointed	31.3.94
12/94	Major review of all water company price limits gets underway	5.4.94
13/94	Parlez vous my language? Water watchdog launches new language line service	5.5.94
14/94	Proposals published for Bournemouth and West Hampshire Water plc to formally replace the two existing water companies	10.5.94
15/94	Water disconnections down by a third - Ian Byatt welcomes latest figures	11.5.94
16/94	1993 Annual Report published: no increase in customer complaints as Ofwat strives to limit price rises	16.6.94
17/94	Bournemouth and West Hampshire Water plc replaces the two existing water companies from this week	29.6.94
18/94	Media invitation: Ian Byatt announces new price limits for water industry	19.7.94
19/94	A new financial climate for the water companies and their customers	28.7.94
20/94	Consumer watchdogs join forces for roadshow	23.8.94
21/94	Appeals against price limits referred to MMC	29.9.94
22/94	Media invitation: Local watchdogs to challenge Ministers over South West bills	17.10.94
23/94	Ofwat publishes paper on future levels of demand and supply for water	10.11.94

24/94 Ofwat reports continuing fall in water disconnections — 15.11.94

25/94 Metering points way to sustainability of water resources — 22.11.94

26/94 Life after the Periodic Review — 29.11.94

27/94 Water regulator urges retention of cost duty on new environment agency — 12.12.94

28/94 Water industry service standards continue to improve — 13.12.94

29/94 Ofwat publishes costs of water delivered and sewage collected — 15.12.94

30/94 Borrowing plays important part in finance of water industry investment — 15.12.94

1995

1/95 Water watchdog launches new textphone service — 30.1.95

2/95 Ofwat strengthens ring fencing protection for customers when water companies plan to diversify — 14.2.95

3/95 Ofwat calls on Government to promote efficient use of sewerage services — 1.3.95

4/95 Rate of increase in bills slows down - average metered bills are falling — 14.3.95

5/95 MMC request extension for dealing with water references — 20.3.95

6/95 Water regulator sounds note of caution to industry on large dividend payouts — 30.3.95

7/95 Ofwat welcomes North West Water's sharing of benefits between customers and shareholders — 30.3.95

8/95 Ofwat welcomes Government decisions on charging methods — 4.4.95

These publications are available free of charge unless otherwise indicated. All publications can be obtained from Ofwat's Library (telephone 0121 625 1373) except where otherwise indicated.

ANNUAL REPORTS

Ofwat annual report 1993 £12.75 ISBN 0 10 241694 X

Annual reports for 1989, 1990, 1991 and 1992 are also available.

Ofwat Customer Service Committee annual reports for 1993-94 are available from the individual CSCs. The 1994-95 CSC annual reports are to be published during June/July 1995.

CONSULTATION PAPERS

Assessing capital values at the Periodic Review: a consultation paper on the framework for reflecting reasonable returns on capital in price limits (November 1992)

Cost of capital (two volumes) (July 1991)

The cost of quality: a strategic assessment of the prospects for future water bills (August 1992)

Paying for growth: a consultation paper on the framework for reflecting the costs of providing for growth (February 1993)

Paying for water: a time for decisions - a consultation paper issued by the Director General of Water Services on future charging policy for water and sewerage services (November 1990)

Information for Regulation (two volumes) (May 1995)

DEAR MANAGING DIRECTOR/REGULATORY DIRECTOR LETTERS

These are copies of letters sent to the Managing Directors or Regulatory Directors of all appointed water companies (August 1989 to date) £3 each (annual subscription April 1995-March 1996 £190)

REPORTS

A better deal for metered customers: a report on tariff rebalancing and improvements in optional metering schemes (March 1994)

Customer preference and willingness to pay for selected water and sewerage services: a summary report to the Office of Water Services by the Flood Hazard Research Centre, Middlesex University, Queensway, Enfield, Middlesex EN3 4SF; telephone 0181 362 5359 (August 1993), £7.50

Financial performance and capital investment of the water companies in England and Wales: 1993-94 report (December 1994). Published annually. 1990-91 report (capital investment only) and 1991-92 and 1992-93 reports also available.

Future charges for water and sewerage companies: the outcome of the Periodic Review (July 1994)

1995-96 Report on tariff structure and charges (May 1995)

Guidelines on debt and disconnection (April 1992)

Guidelines on debt and disconnection: report on company progress 1992-93 (May 1993)

Guidelines on optional metering (May 1992)

Guidelines on services for disabled and elderly customers (September 1991)

Levels of Service for the water industry of England and Wales 1993-94 (December 1994) Published annually; 1989-90, 1990-91, 1991-92 and 1992-93 reports also available.

Meter installation report: a survey of customers in the water metering trials areas (March 1992)

Ofwat complaints procedure (August 1994) Also available in Welsh from CSC for Wales.

Opting for a meter: a report on water company optional metering schemes (March 1994) £3

Paying for quality: the political perspective (July 1993)

Paying for water: the way ahead - the Director General's conclusions (December 1991)

Services for elderly or disabled customers: a report on companies' progress in implementing Ofwat guidelines (September 1993)

Setting price limits for water and sewerage services: executive overview. The framework and approach to the 1994 Periodic Review (November 1993). Full report also available.

The cost of water delivered and sewage collected 1993-94 (December 1994) and addendum. Published annually. 1991-92 (water delivered only) and 1992-93 reports also available.

The customer viewpoint: a quantitative survey (MORI report) (May 1992), £5

The distributional effects of different methods of charging households for water and sewerage services: a report prepared for Ofwat by the Institute for Fiscal Studies (August 1993), £5

The social impact of water metering (August 1992) Summary - free; First report - £5; First report: tables - £5; Second report - £10

The UK water industry: water services and costs 1993-94 (March 1995) Sponsored by Ofwat and published by the Public Finance Foundation, 3 Robert Street, London WC2N 6BH; tel 0171 895 8823 £25, ISBN 0 85299 670 5

MISCELLANEOUS

AMP2 manual: strategic business plan (two volumes) (October 1992), £50 (£100 including amendments which will be issued irregularly).

Definitions manual annex (November 1992), £50 (£100 including amendments which will be issued irregularly).

Water supply, sewage disposal and the water environment: a guide to the regulatory system (November 1994)

REGULATORY ACCOUNTING GUIDELINES (RAGS)

RAG 1 Guideline for accounting for current costs. [version 1.02] (May 1992), £3

RAG2 Classification of infrastructure expenditure. [version 2.01] (February 1991), £3

RAG 3 Guideline for the contents of regulatory accounts. [version 3.02 & 3.03] (May 1992), £3

RAG 4 Guideline for the analysis of operating costs and assets. [version 4.01] (June 1992), £3

RAG 5 Transfer pricing in the water industry. [version 5.01] (March 1994), £3

INFORMATION NOTES

1. Monitoring company performance: the July return (revised March 1993)
2. Financing of major environmental improvements (revised January 1993)
3. Why water bills are rising and how they are controlled (revised March 1993)
4. Guaranteed standards scheme (revised September 1994)
5. Comparing company performance (revised January 1993)
6. Controls on land disposal (revised February 1992)
7. Charges for a new connection to the mains or sewer (revised September 1994)
8. The K factor - what it is and how it can be changed (revised September 1994)
9. Diversification by water companies (revised April 1992)
10. Increasing competition in the water industry (April 1992)
11. First time rural sewerage (August 1992)
12. Water pressure (revised January 1993)
13. Water delivered (revised January 1993)
14. Responsibility for water and sewerage pipes (revised August 1992)
16. Water charges and company profits (revised January 1993)

17. 1994 review of water company charging limits: the Periodic Review (revised December 1993)

18. Privatisation and history of the water industry (February 1993)

19. Tariff rebalancing between measured and unmeasured customers (August 1994)

20. Principles for developing water charging policies (June 1994)

21. Trade effluent appeals (May 1993)

22. Pipeline powers on private land (December 1993)

23. Introducing the licence (February 1994)

24. The urban waste water treatment directive (February 1994)

25. Water bill increases 1994-95 (February 1994)

26. The role of the regulator (March 1994)

27. Paying by meter (March 1994)

28. Reporters, auditors and valuers (April 1994)

29. The structure of the water and sewerage industries in England and Wales(August 1994)

30. Water industry referrals on price limits to the Monopolies and Mergers Commission (August 1994)

LEAFLETS

A new financial climate for the water industry: a better deal for customers (August 1994)

Customer Service Committees: a water watchdog role for you? A guide to the functions of CSCs and their members (March 1995). Also available in large print and on tape.

Ofwat and the business customer (March 1995)

Paying for water: the way ahead - the Director General's conclusions (December 1991)

Protecting the interests of water customers (March 1995) Also available in large print and in Welsh.

The voice of water customers: Ofwat National Customer Council (March 1995)

Water and sewerage bills 1995-96 (March 1995). Published annually.

Water and sewerage: how we can help if you have a complaint (August 1994). Also available in Welsh from CSC for Wales.

Water and you: this guide illustrates the costs of everyday use of water and sewerage based on an average bill for 1995-96 (April 1995). Published annually.

Water facts & figures 1994 (October 1994). Published annually.

OCCASIONAL PAPERS

Future levels of demand and supply for water (November 1994), £3

RESEARCH PAPERS

1. Comparing the cost of water delivered: initial research into the impact of operating conditions on company costs (March 1993), £3

2. Modelling water costs 1992-93: further research into the impact of operating conditions on company costs (three volumes) (December 1993), £3

3. Modelling sewerage costs 1992-93: research into the impact of operating conditions on the costs of the sewerage network (three volumes) (January 1994), £3

4. Modelling sewage treatment costs 1992-93: research into the impact of operating conditions on the costs of the sewage treatment (three volumes) (January 1994), £3

5. Comparing sewerage service operating expenditure: an overview into the impact of operating conditions on companies' operating expenditure in 1992-93 (February 1994)

SPEECHES

Speeches made by both the Director General of Water Services, Ian Byatt and the Deputy Director General, Alan Booker, £3 each. A list is available from the Library.

TAPES

All about Ofwat. Produced for the visually disadvantaged and caring and advice agencies (September 1992). Also available in Welsh.

A water watchdog role for you? Explains the role of Ofwat's ten regional Customer Service Committees and how to become a CSC member (January 1993)

VIDEOS

The visit: Ofwat and a forceful mother-in-law help solve a young couple's problem with their water bill (November 1991) (15 mins). This VHS PAL video is available on free loan or for purchase at £5 per copy.

INDEPENDENT AUDITORS AND REPORTERS

	Auditors	Reporters
Water and sewerage companies		
Anglian Water Services Ltd	Price Waterhouse	W S Atkins*
Dŵr Cymru Cyfyngedig	Coopers & Lybrand	Halcrow Management Sciences
Northumbrian Water Ltd	Coopers & Lybrand	Binnie & Partners
North West Water Ltd	Price Waterhouse	Halcrow Management Sciences
Severn Trent Water Ltd	Price Waterhouse	Halcrow Management Sciences
Southern Water Services Ltd	Coopers & Lybrand	W S Atkins
South West Water Services Ltd	Price Waterhouse	W S Atkins
Thames Water Utilities Ltd	Coopers & Lybrand	W S Atkins
Wessex Water Services Ltd	Coopers & Lybrand	Halcrow Management Sciences
Yorkshire Water Services Ltd	Price Waterhouse	W S Atkins (1994) Binnie & Partners (1995)
Water only companies		
Bournemouth & West Hampshire Water plc	Price Waterhouse	Lichfield Management Sciences
Bristol Water plc	Coopers & Lybrand	W S Atkins
Cambridge Water Company	BDO Binder Hamlyn	Pick Everard
Chester Waterworks Company	Saffrey Champness	Halcrow Management Sciences
Cholderton & District Water Company Ltd**	B Johnson Esq	
East Surrey Water plc	KPMG Peat Marwick	Binnie & Partners
Essex and Suffolk Water plc	Arthur Andersen & Co	Halcrow Management Sciences
Folkestone & Dover Water Services Ltd	Coopers & Lybrand	Montgomery Watson Sciences
Hartlepool Water plc	Clarke Whitehill	Halcrow Management Sciences
Mid Kent Water plc	Arthur Anderson & Co	Halcrow Management Sciences
Mid Southern Water plc	Coopers & Lybrand	Halcrow Management Sciences
North East Water plc	Arthur Andersen & Co	Halcrow Management Sciences
North Surrey Water plc	Coopers & Lybrand	Montgomery Watson
Portsmouth Water plc	Grant Thornton	Rofe, Kennard & Lapworth
South East Water Ltd	Coopers & Lybrand	Halcrow Management Sciences
South Staffordshire Water plc	Arthur Andersen & Co	Halcrow Management Sciences
Sutton District Water plc	BDO Binder Hamlyn	Halcrow Management Sciences
Tendring Hundred Water Services Ltd	Coopers & Lybrand	Montgomery Wilson
Three Valleys Water plc	Coopers & Lybrand	W S Atkins
Wrexham Water plc	Saffrey Champness	Halcrow Management Sciences
York Waterworks plc	Garbutt & Elliott	Halcrow Management Sciences

*   Anglian Water Services is in the process of changing its reporter to Binnie & Partners

**   Cholderton & District Water Company is an exceptionally small company and does not provide information

BOURNEMOUTH & WEST HAMPSHIRE WATER PLC

Head Office Address: George Jessel House

Francis Avenue

Bournemouth BH11 8NB

Telephone: 01202 591111

BRISTOL WATER PLC

Head Office Address: PO Box 218

Bridgwater Road

Bristol BS99 7AU

Telephone: 0117 966 5881

CAMBRIDGE WATER COMPANY

Head Office Address: 41 Rustat Road

Cambridge CB1 3QS

Telephone: 01223 403000

CHESTER WATERWORKS COMPANY

Head Office Address: Aqua House

45 Boughton

Chester CH3 5AU

Telephone: 01244 320501

CHOLDERTON & DISTRICT WATER COMPANY LTD

Head Office Address: Estate Office

Cholderton

Salisbury

Wiltshire SP4 0DR

Telephone: 01980 629203

EAST SURREY WATER PLC

Head Office Address: London Road

Redhill

Surrey RH1 1LJ

Telephone: 01737 772000

ESSEX & SUFFOLK WATER PLC

Head Office Address: Hall Street

Chelmsford

Essex CM2 0HH

Telephone: 01245 491234

FOLKESTONE & DOVER WATER SERVICES LTD

Head Office Address: Cherry Garden Lane
Folkestone
Kent CT19 4QB

Telephone: 01303 276951

HARTLEPOOL WATER PLC

Head Office Address: 3 Lancaster Road
Hartlepool
TS24 8LW

Telephone: 01429 274405

MID KENT WATER PLC

Head Office Address: PO Box 45
High Street
Snodland
Kent ME6 5AH

Telephone: 01634 240313

MID SOUTHERN WATER PLC

Head Office Address: Frimley Green
Camberley
Surrey GU16 6HZ

Telephone: 01252 835031

NORTH EAST WATER PLC

Head Office Address: PO Box 10
Allendale Road
Newcastle upon Tyne
NE6 2SW

Telephone: 0191 265 4144

NORTH SURREY WATER LTD

Head Office Address: Millis House
The Causeway
Staines
Middlesex TW18 3BX

Telephone: 01784 455464

PORTSMOUTH WATER PLC

Head Office Address: PO Box 8

West Street

Havant

Hants PO9 1LG

Telephone: 01705 499888

SOUTH EAST WATER LTD

Head Office Address: 14 Upperton Road

Eastbourne

East Sussex BN21 1EP

Telephone: 01323 411411

SOUTH STAFFORDSHIRE WATER PLC

Head Office Address: Green Lane

Walsall

West Midlands WS2 7PD

Telephone: 01922 38282

SUTTON DISTRICT WATER PLC

Head Office Address: 59 Gander Green Lane

Cheam

Sutton

Surrey SM1 2EW

Telephone: 0181 643 8050

TENDRING HUNDRED WATER SERVICES LTD

Head Office Address: Mill Hill

Manningtree

Essex CO11 2AZ

Telephone: 01206 392155

THREE VALLEYS WATER PLC

Head Office Address: PO Box 48

Bishop's Rise

Hatfield

Herts AL10 9HL

Telephone: 01707 268111

WREXHAM WATER PLC

Head Office Address: Packsaddle

Wrexham Road

Rhostyllen

Wrexham

Clwyd

North Wales LL14 4DS

Telephone: 01978 846946

YORK WATERWORKS PLC

Head Office Address: Lendal Tower

York YO1 2DL

Telephone: 01904 622171

APPENDIX · APPENDIX 7

ANGLIAN WATER SERVICES LTD

Head Office Address: Compass House

Chivers Way

Histon

Cambridgeshire CB4 4ZY

Telephone: 01223 372000

DŴR CYMRU CYFYNGEDIG (WELSH WATER)

Head Office Address: Plas-y-Ffynnon

Cambrian Way

Brecon

Powys LD3 7HP

Telephone: 01874 623181

NORTH WEST WATER LTD

Head Office Address: Dawson House

Great Sankey

Warrington WA5 3LW

Telephone: 01925 234000

NORTHUMBRIAN WATER LTD

Head Office Address: Abbey Road

Pity Me

Durham DH1 5FJ

Telephone: 0191 383 2222

SEVERN TRENT WATER LTD

Head Office Address: 2297 Coventry Road

Sheldon

Birmingham B26 3PU

Telephone: 0121 722 4000

SOUTH WEST WATER SERVICES LTD

Head Office Address: Peninsula House

Rydon Lane

Exeter EX2 7HR

Telephone: 01392 446688

SOUTHERN WATER SERVICES LTD

Head Office Address: Southern House
Yeoman Road
Worthing
Sussex BN13 3NX

Telephone: 01903 264444

THAMES WATER UTILITIES LTD

Head Office Address: Nugent House
Vastern Road
Reading RG1 8DB

Telephone: 01734 591 159

WESSEX WATER SERVICES LTD

Head Office Address: Wessex House
Passage Street
Bristol BS2 0JQ

Telephone: 0117 9290611

YORKSHIRE WATER SERVICES LTD

Head Office Address: West Riding House
67 Albion Street
Leeds LS1 5AA

Telephone: 0113 244 8201

Printed in the United Kingdom for HMSO
Dd 5064508, 6/95, C30, 51-8465, 39462, Ord 326600